GRAMMAR OF ORNAMENT

THE
WADSWORTH
LIBRARY
GENESEO
N.Y.

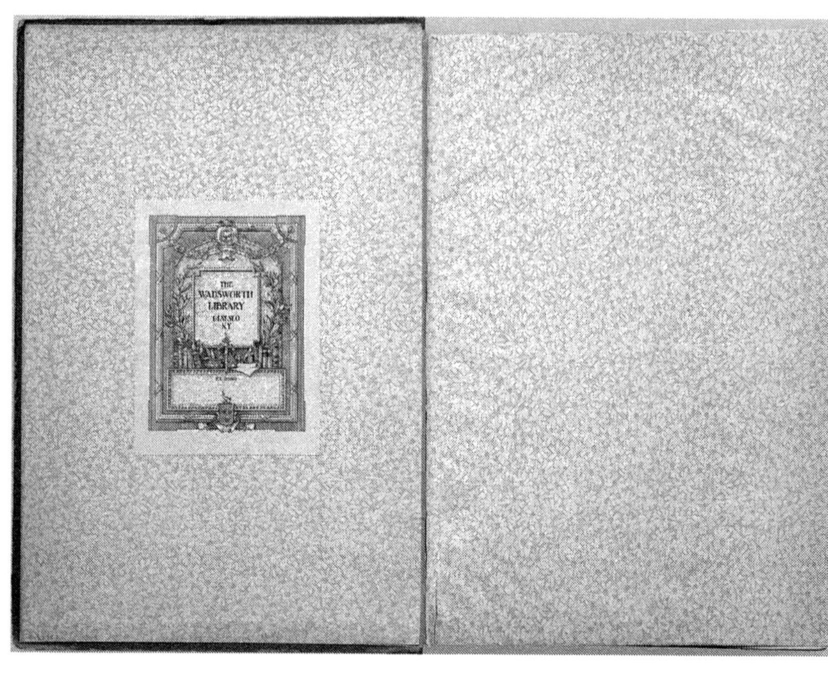

The Grammar of Ornament

THE

GRAMMAR OF ORNAMENT

BY

OWEN JONES.

ILLUSTRATED BY EXAMPLES
FROM VARIOUS STYLES OF ORNAMENT.

ONE HUNDRED AND TWELVE PLATES.

LONDON
PUBLISHED BY DAY AND SON, LIMITED,
GATE STREET, LINCOLN'S INN FIELDS.

PREFACE TO THE FOLIO EDITION.

It would be far beyond the limits of the powers of any one individual to attempt to gather together illustrations of the innumerable and ever-varying phases of Ornamental Art. It would be barely possible if undertaken by a government, and even then it would be too voluminous to be generally useful. All, therefore, that I have proposed to myself in forming the collection which I have ventured to call the *Grammar of Ornament*, has been to select a few of the most prominent types in certain styles closely connected with each other, and in which certain general laws appeared to reign independently of the individual peculiarities of each. I have ventured to hope that, in thus bringing into immediate juxtaposition the many forms of beauty which every style of ornament presents, I might aid in arresting that unfortunate tendency of our time to be content with copying, whilst the fashion lasts, the forms peculiar to any bygone age, without attempting to ascertain, generally completely ignoring, the peculiar circumstances which rendered an ornament beautiful, because it was appropriate, and which as expressive of other wants, when thus transplanted, as entirely fails.

It is more than probable that the first result of sending forth to the world this collection will be seriously to increase this dangerous tendency, and that many will be content to borrow from the past those forms of beauty which have not already been used up *ad nauseam*. It has been my desire to arrest this tendency, and to awaken a higher ambition.

If the student will but endeavour to search out the thoughts which have been expressed in so many different languages, he may assuredly hope to find an ever-gushing fountain in place of a half-filled stagnant reservoir.

In the following chapters I have endeavoured to establish these main facts,—

First. That whenever any style of ornament commands universal admiration, it will always be found to be in accordance with the laws which regulate the distribution of form in nature.

Secondly. That however varied the manifestations in accordance with these laws, the leading ideas on which they are based are very few.

Thirdly. That the modifications and developments which have taken place from one style to another have been caused by a sudden throwing off of some fixed trammel, which set thought free for a time, till the new idea, like the old, became again fixed, to give birth in its turn to fresh inventions.

Lastly. I have endeavoured to show, in the twentieth chapter, that the future progress of Ornamental Art may be best secured by engrafting on the experience of the past the knowledge we may obtain by a return to Nature for fresh inspiration. To attempt to build up theories of art, or to form a style, independently of the past, would be an act of supreme folly. It would be at once to reject the experiences and accumulated knowledge of thousands of years. On the contrary, we should regard as our inheritance all the successful labours of the past, not blindly following them, but employing them simply as guides to find the true path.

In taking leave of the subject, and finally surrendering it to the judgment of the public, I am fully aware that the collection is very far from being complete; there are many gaps which each artist, however, may readily fill up for himself. My chief aim, to place side by side types of such styles as might best serve

as landmarks and aids to the student in his onward path, has, I trust, been fulfilled.

It remains for me to offer my acknowledgment to all those friends who have kindly assisted me in the undertaking.

In the formation of the Egyptian Collection I received much valuable assistance from Mr. J. Bonomi, and from Mr. James Wild, who has also contributed the materials for the Arabian Collection, his long residence in Cairo having afforded him the opportunity of forming a very large collection of Cairene Ornament, of which the portion contained in this work can give but an imperfect idea, and which I trust he may some day be encouraged to publish in a complete form.

I am indebted to Mr. T. T. Bury for the plate of Stained Glass. From Mr. C. J. Richardson I obtained the principal portion of the materials of the Elizabethan Collection; from Mr. J. B. Waring, those of the Byzantine, and I am also indebted to him for the very valuable essays on Byzantine and Elizabethan Ornament. Mr. J. O. Westwood having directed especial attention to the Ornament of the Celtic races, has assisted in the Celtic Collection, and written the very remarkable history and exposition of the style.

Mr. C. Dresser, of Marlborough House, has provided the interesting plate No. 8 of the twentieth chapter, exhibiting the geometrical arrangement of natural flowers.

My colleague at the Crystal Palace, M. Digby Wyatt, has enriched the work with his admirable essays on the Ornament of the Renaissance and the Italian periods.

Whenever the material has been gathered from published sources, it has been acknowledged in the body of the work.

The remainder of the drawings have been chiefly executed by my pupils, Mr. Albert Warren and Mr. Charles Aubert, who, with Mr. Stubbs, have reduced the whole of the original drawings, and prepared them for publication.

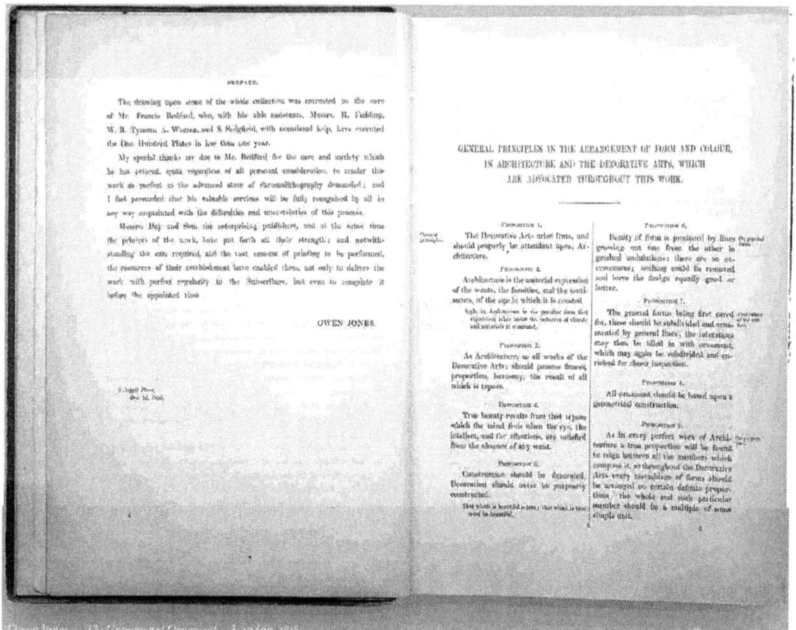

PREFACE.

The drawing upon stone of the whole collection was entrusted to the care of Mr. Francis Bedford, who, with his able assistants, Messrs. H. Fielding, W. R. Tymms, A. Warren, and S. Sedgfield, with occasional help, have executed the One Hundred Plates in less than one year.

My special thanks are due to Mr. Bedford for the care and anxiety which he has evinced, quite regardless of all personal consideration, to render this work as perfect as the advanced state of chromolithography demanded; and I feel persuaded that his valuable services will be fully recognised by all in any way acquainted with the difficulties and uncertainties of this process.

Messrs. Day and Son, the enterprising publishers, and at the same time the printers of the work, have put forth all their strength; and notwithstanding the care required, and the vast amount of printing to be performed, the resources of their establishment have enabled them, not only to deliver the work with perfect regularity to the Subscribers, but even to complete it before the appointed time.

OWEN JONES.

9 Argyll Place,
Dec. 15, 1856.

4

GENERAL PRINCIPLES IN THE ARRANGEMENT OF FORM AND COLOUR, IN ARCHITECTURE AND THE DECORATIVE ARTS, WHICH ARE ADVOCATED THROUGHOUT THIS WORK.

PROPOSITION 1.

The Decorative Arts arise from, and should properly be attendant upon, Architecture.

PROPOSITION 2.

Architecture is the material expression of the wants, the faculties, and the sentiments, of the age in which it is created.

Style in Architecture is the peculiar form that expression takes under the influence of climate and materials at command.

PROPOSITION 3.

As Architecture, so all works of the Decorative Arts, should possess fitness, proportion, harmony, the result of all which is repose.

PROPOSITION 4.

True beauty results from that repose which the mind feels when the eye, the intellect, and the affections, are satisfied from the absence of any want.

PROPOSITION 5.

Construction should be decorated. Decoration should never be purposely constructed.

That which is beautiful is true; that which is true must be beautiful.

PROPOSITION 6.

Beauty of form is produced by lines growing out one from the other in gradual undulations: there are no excrescences; nothing could be removed and leave the design equally good or better.

PROPOSITION 7.

The general forms being first cared for, these should be subdivided and ornamented by general lines; the interstices may then be filled in with ornament, which may again be subdivided and enriched for closer inspection.

PROPOSITION 8.

All ornament should be based upon a geometrical construction.

PROPOSITION 9.

As in every perfect work of Architecture a true proportion will be found to reign between all the members which compose it, so throughout the Decorative Arts every assemblage of forms should be arranged on certain definite proportions; the whole and each particular member should be a multiple of some simple unit.

5

Owen Jones. *The Grammar of Ornament*. London, 1856.

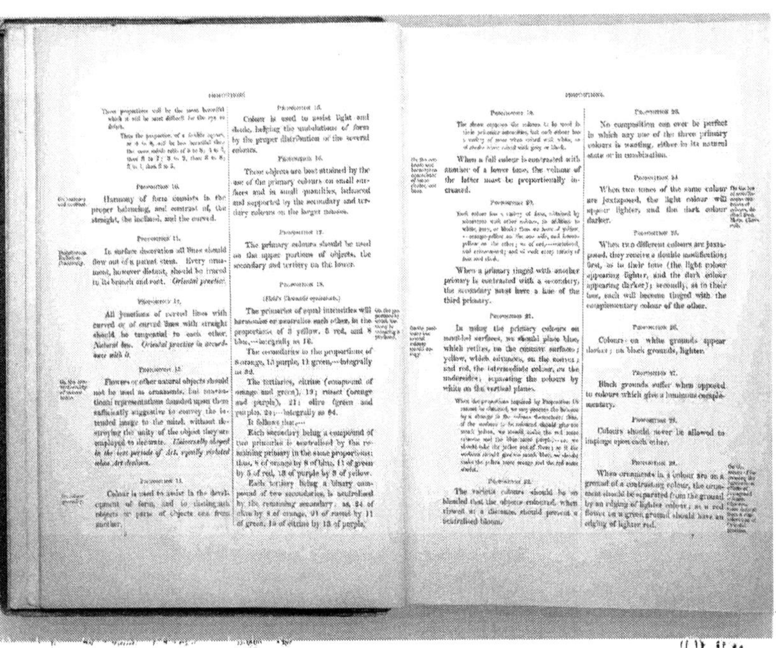

These proportions will be the most beautiful which it will be most difficult for the eye to detect.

Thus the proportion of a double square, or 4 to 8, will be less beautiful than the more subtle ratio of 5 to 8; 3 to 6, than 3 to 7; 3 to 9, than 3 to 8; 3 to 4, than 3 to 5.

PROPOSITION 10.

Harmony of form consists in the proper balancing, and contrast of, the straight, the inclined, and the curved.

PROPOSITION 11.

In surface decoration all lines should flow out of a parent stem. Every ornament, however distant, should be traced to its branch and root. *Oriental practice.*

PROPOSITION 12.

All junctions of curved lines with curved or of curved lines with straight should be tangential to each other. *Natural law. Oriental practice in accordance with it.*

PROPOSITION 13.

Flowers or other natural objects should not be used as ornaments, but conventional representations founded upon them sufficiently suggestive to convey the intended image to the mind, without destroying the unity of the object they are employed to decorate. *Universally obeyed in the best periods of Art, equally violated when Art declines.*

PROPOSITION 14.

Colour is used to assist in the development of form, and to distinguish objects or parts of objects one from another.

PROPOSITION 15.

Colour is used to assist light and shade, helping the undulations of form by the proper distribution of the several colours.

PROPOSITION 16.

These objects are best attained by the use of the primary colours on small surfaces and in small quantities, balanced and supported by the secondary and tertiary colours on the larger masses.

PROPOSITION 17.

The primary colours should be used on the upper portions of objects, the secondary and tertiary on the lower.

PROPOSITION 18.

(Field's Chromatic equivalents.)

The primaries of equal intensities will harmonise or neutralise each other, in the proportions of 3 yellow, 5 red, and 8 blue,—integrally as 16.

The secondaries in the proportions of 8 orange, 13 purple, 11 green,—integrally as 32.

The tertiaries, citrine (compound of orange and green), 19; russet (orange and purple), 21; olive (green and purple), 24;—integrally as 64.

It follows that,—

Each secondary being a compound of two primaries is neutralised by the remaining primary in the same proportions: thus, 8 of orange by 8 of blue, 11 of green by 5 of red, 13 of purple by 3 of yellow.

Each tertiary being a binary compound of two secondaries, is neutralised by the remaining secondary: as, 24 of olive by 8 of orange, 21 of russet by 11 of green, 19 of citrine by 13 of purple.

PROPOSITION 19.

The above supposes the colours to be used in their prismatic intensities, but each colour has a variety of tones when mixed with white, or of shades when mixed with grey or black.

When a full colour is contrasted with another of a lower tone, the volume of the latter must be proportionally increased.

PROPOSITION 20.

When a primary tinged with another primary is contrasted with a secondary, the secondary must have a hue of the third primary.

PROPOSITION 21.

In using the primary colours on moulded surfaces, we should place blue, which retires, on the concave surfaces; yellow, which advances, on the convex; and red, the intermediate colour, on the undersides; separating the colours by white on the vertical planes.

When the proportions required by Proposition 18 cannot be obtained, we may procure the balance by a change in the colours themselves: thus, if the surfaces to be coloured should give too much yellow, we should make the red more crimson and the blue more purple,—i.e. we should take the yellow out of them; so if the surfaces should give too much blue, we should make the yellow more orange and the red more scarlet.

PROPOSITION 22.

The various colours should be so blended that the objects coloured, when viewed at a distance, should present a neutralised bloom.

PROPOSITION 23.

No composition can ever be perfect in which any one of the three primary colours is wanting, either in its natural state or in combination.

PROPOSITION 24.

When two tones of the same colour are juxtaposed, the light colour will appear lighter, and the dark colour darker.

PROPOSITION 25.

When two different colours are juxtaposed, they receive a double modification; first, as to their tone (the light colour appearing lighter, and the dark colour appearing darker); secondly, as to their hue, each will become tinged with the complementary colour of the other.

PROPOSITION 26.

Colours on white grounds appear darker; on black grounds, lighter.

PROPOSITION 27.

Black grounds suffer when opposed to colours which give a luminous complementary.

PROPOSITION 28.

Colours should never be allowed to impinge upon each other.

PROPOSITION 29.

When ornaments in a colour are on a ground of a contrasting colour, the ornament should be separated from the ground by an edging of lighter colour; as a red flower on a green ground should have an edging of lighter red.

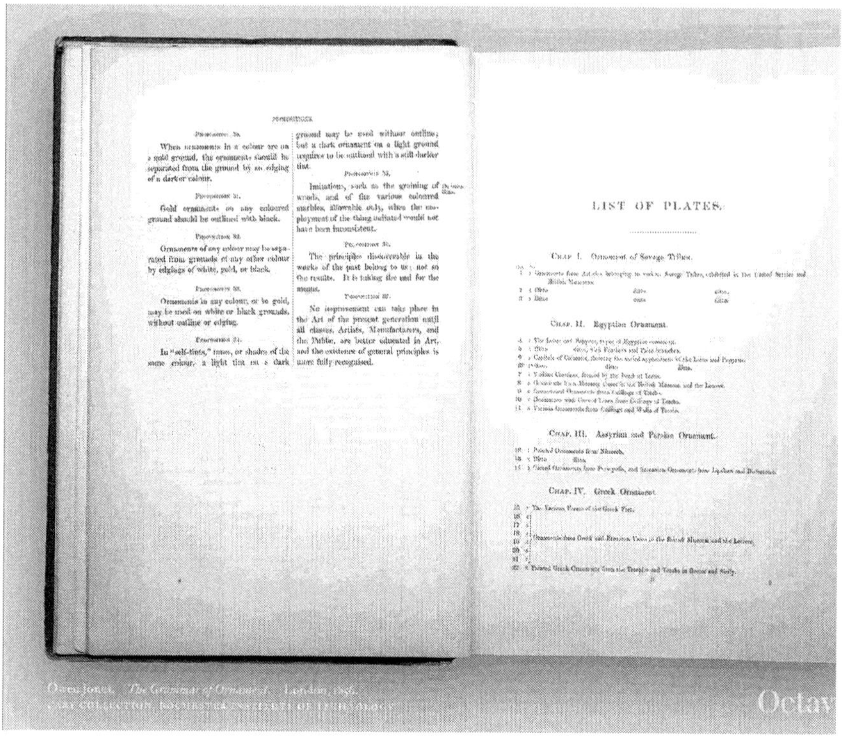

When ornaments in a colour are on a gold ground, the ornaments should be separated from the ground by an edging of a darker colour.

Gold ornaments on any coloured ground should be outlined with black.

Ornaments of any colour may be separated from grounds of any other colour by edgings of white, gold, or black.

Ornaments in any colour, or in gold, may be used on white or black grounds, without outline or edging.

In "self-tints," tints, or shades of the same colour, a light tint on a dark ground may be used without outline; but a dark ornament on a light ground requires to be outlined with a still darker tint.

Imitations, such as the graining of woods, and of the various coloured marbles, allowable only, when the employment of the thing imitated would not have been inconsistent.

The principles discoverable in the works of the past belong to us; not so the results. It is taking the end for the means.

No improvement can take place in the Art of the present generation until all classes, Artists, Manufacturers, and the Public, are better educated in Art, and the existence of general principles is more fully recognised.

LIST OF PLATES.

CHAP. I. Ornament of Savage Tribes.

CHAP. II. Egyptian Ornament.

CHAP. III. Assyrian and Persian Ornament.

CHAP. IV. Greek Ornament.

[illegible]

Chap. V. Pompeian Ornament.

Plate No.

23 1 Collection of Borders from different Villas in Pompeii.
24 2 Ditto Pilasters and [illegible] ditto.
25 3 Mosaics from Pompeii and the Museum at Naples.

Chap. VI. Roman Ornament.

26 1 Roman Ornaments from Casts in the Crystal Palace.
27 2 Ditto from the "Museo Borbonico."

Chap. VII. Byzantine Ornament.

28 1 Carved Byzantine Ornaments.
29 2 Painted ditto.
29* 2* Ditto ditto.
30 3 Mosaics.

Chap. VIII. Arabian Ornament.

31 1 Arabian Ornaments of the Ninth Century from Cairo.
32 2 Ditto [illegible] Century ditto.
33 3 Ditto ditto ditto.
34 4 Portion of an Illuminated Copy of the "Koran."
35 5 Mosaics from Walls and Pavements from Houses at Cairo.

Chap. IX. Turkish Ornament.

36 1 Ornaments in Relief from Mosques, Tombs, and Fountains at Constantinople.
37 2 Painted Ornament from the Mosque of Soliman at Constantinople.
38 3 Decoration of the Dome of the Tomb of Soliman I. at Constantinople.

Chap. X. Moresque Ornament from the Alhambra.

39 1 Varieties of Interlaced Ornaments.
40 2 Spandrils of Arches.
41 3 Lozenge Diapers.
41* 3* Ditto ditto.
42 4 Square Diapers.
42* 4* Ditto ditto.
42† 4† Ditto ditto.
43 5 Mosaics.

Chap. XI. Persian Ornament.

44 1 Ornaments from Persian MSS. in the British Museum.
45 2 Ditto ditto.
46 3 Ditto ditto.
47 4 From a Persian Manufacturer's Pattern-Book, South Kensington Museum.
47* 4* Ditto ditto ditto.
48 5 From a Persian MS. South Kensington Museum.

Chap. XII. Indian Ornament.

Plate No.

49 1 Ornaments from Metal-work from the Exhibition of 1851.
50 2 }
51 3 } Ditto from Embroidered and Woven Fabrics and Paintings on Vases exhibited in the Indian Collection in 1851, now at South Kensington Museum.
52 4 }
53 5 }
53* 5* } Specimens of Painted Lacquer-work from the Collection at the India House.
54 6 }
54* 6* }
55 7 Ornaments from Woven and Embroidered Fabrics and Painted Boxes exhibited at Paris in 1855.

Chap. XIII. Hindoo Ornament.

56 1 Ornaments from a Statue at the Asiatic Society's House.
57 2 From the Collection at the Crystal Palace, Sydenham.
58 3 From the Collection at the India House.

Chap. XIV. Chinese Ornament.

59 1 }
60 2 } Chinese Ornaments painted on Porcelain, and on Wood, and from Woven Fabrics.
61 3 }
62 4 Conventional Renderings of Fruits and Flowers.

Chap. XV. Celtic Ornament.

63 1 Lapidary Ornamentation.
64 2 Interlaced Styles.
65 3 Spiral, Diagonal, Zoomorphic, and later Anglo-Saxon Ornament.

Chap. XVI. Mediæval Ornament.

66 1 Conventional Leaves and Flowers from Illuminated MSS.
67 2 Borders from Illuminated MSS. and Paintings.
67* 2* Ditto ditto ditto.
68 3 Diapers from Illuminated MSS. and Backgrounds of Pictures.
69 4 Stained Glass of various periods.
69* 4* Ditto ditto.
70 5 Encaustic Tiles, ditto.

Illuminated MSS.

71 1 Portions of Illuminated MSS. of the Twelfth and Thirteenth Centuries.
72 2 Ditto ditto Thirteenth and Fourteenth ditto.
73 3 Ditto ditto Fourteenth and Fifteenth ditto.

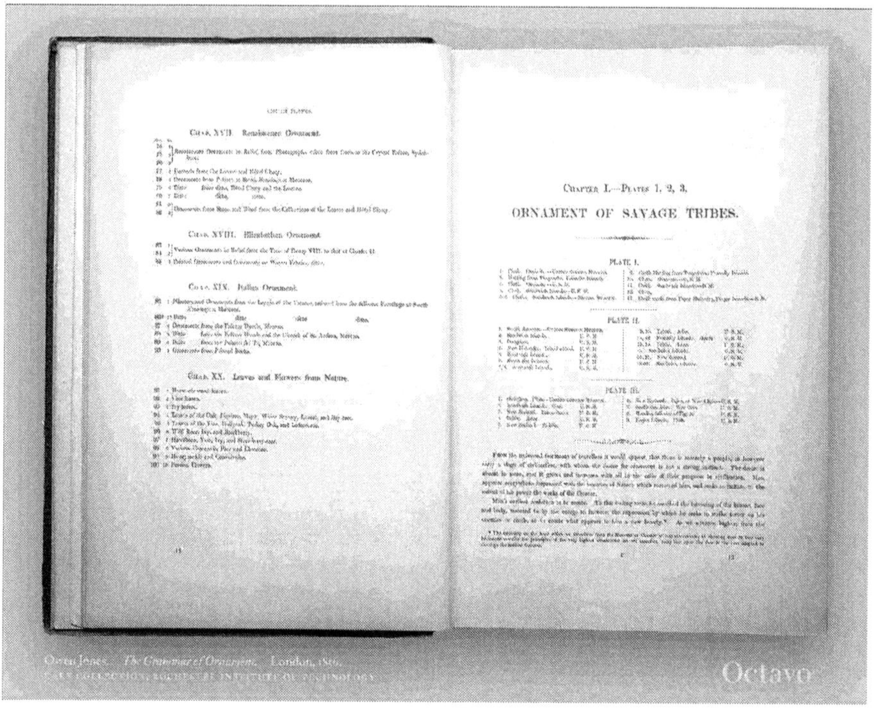

Chap. XVII. Renaissance Ornament.
Chap. XVIII. Elizabethan Ornament.
Chap. XIX. Italian Ornament.
Chap. XX. Leaves and Flowers from Nature.
Chapter I.—Plates 1, 2, 3.
ORNAMENT OF SAVAGE TRIBES.
PLATE I.
PLATE II.
PLATE III.
Owen Jones. The Grammar of Ornament. London, 1856.
Octavo

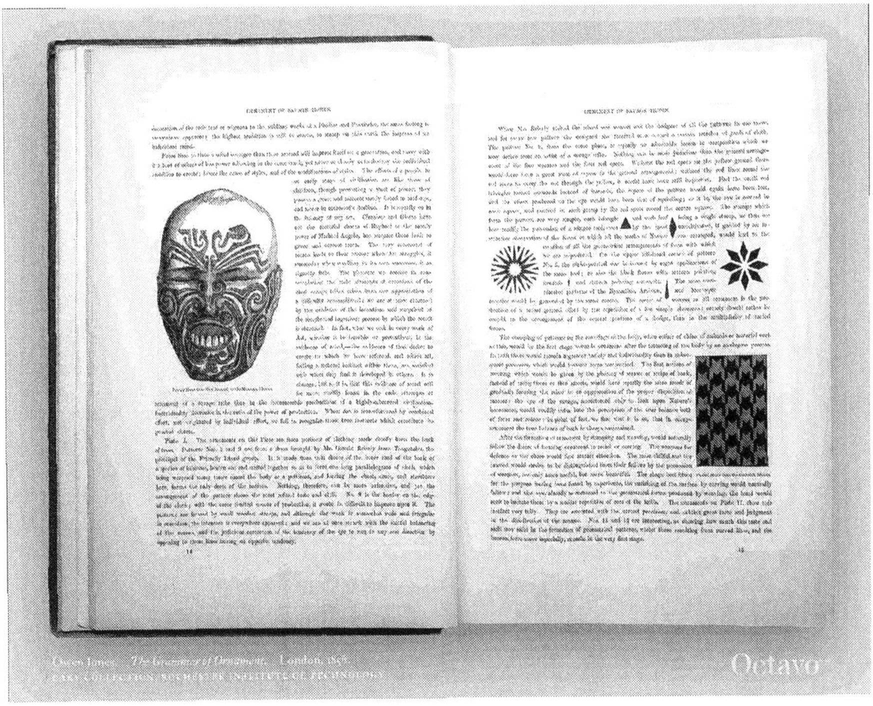
Octavo

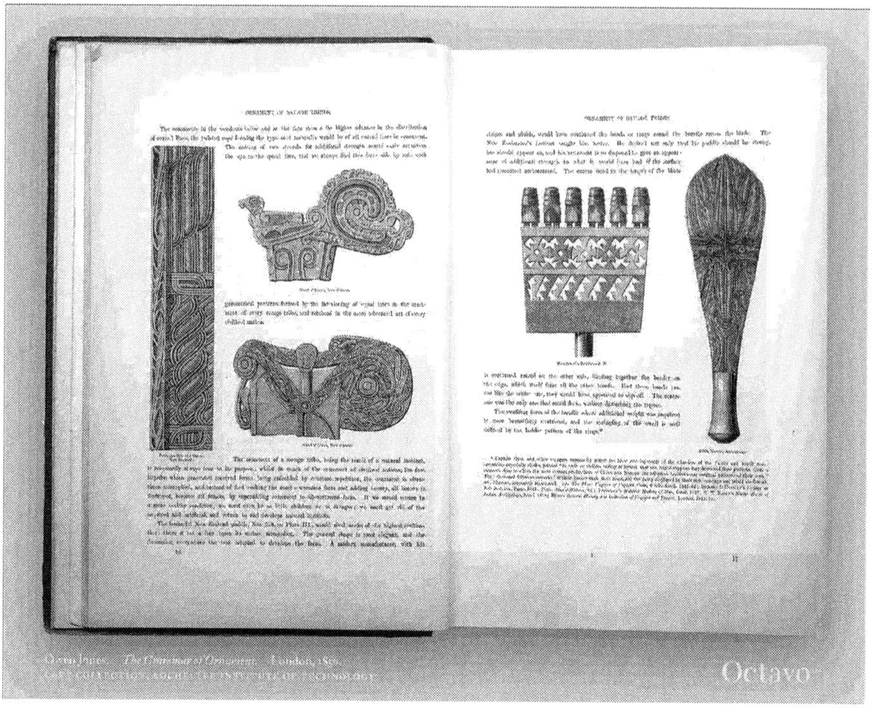
Owen Jones. The Grammar of Ornament. London,
CARY COLLECTION, ROCHESTER INSTITUTE OF TECHNOLOGY
Octavo

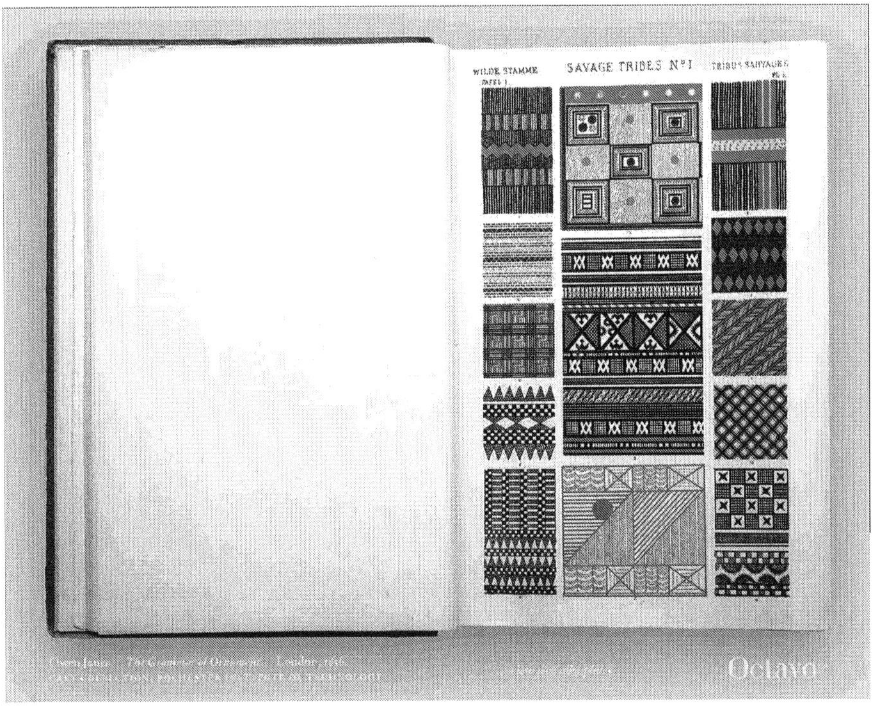
WILDE STAMME
SAVAGE TRIBES Nº 1
Owen Jones · The Grammar of Ornament · London, 1856.
Octavo

WILDE STAMME
SAVAGE TRIBES Nº 2
TRIBUS SAUVAGES
Octavo

SAVAGE TRIBES No 3.
Owen Jones. *The Grammar of Ornament.* London, 1856.
Octavo

Chapter II.—Plates 4, 5, 6, 6*, 7, 8, 9, 10, 11.

EGYPTIAN ORNAMENT.

PLATE IV.

1. The Lotus, [illegible]
2. Egyptian representation of the Lotus.
3. Another, in a different stage of growth.
4. [illegible]
5. [illegible]
6. [illegible]
7. [illegible]
8. [illegible]
9. Another, in a less advanced stage of growth.
10. Egyptian representation of the Papyrus Plant; [illegible]
11. [illegible]
12. A combination of the Lotus and Papyrus, [illegible]
13. Egyptian representation of the Lotus and Buds.
14, 15. Representation of the Papyrus, [illegible]
16. Representation of Plants growing in the Desert.
17. Representation of the Lotus and Papyrus growing on the Nile.
18. Another variety of Desert Plants.

PLATE V.

1. [illegible]
2. [illegible]
3. [illegible]
4. [illegible]
5. Ditto.
6. Fan.
7. Royal Head-dress.
8. Ditto.
9. Representation of a species of Lotus.
10. The blue Lotus.
11. [illegible]
12. Another variety.
13, 14, 15. Gold and enamelled [illegible] in the Form of the Lotus.
16. [illegible] with the Lotus and the [illegible], representing the Divinity.
17. Ditto, another variety.
18, 19. Boats made of Papyrus Plants bound together.

PLATE VI.

1. Capital of the large Columns of the Temple of Luxor, Thebes, [illegible]
2. Capital of the smaller Columns of the [illegible], Thebes, [illegible]
3. [illegible]

PLATE VI.

PLATE VII.

PLATE VIII.

PLATE IX.

PLATE X.

PLATE XI.

EGYPTIAN ORNAMENT.

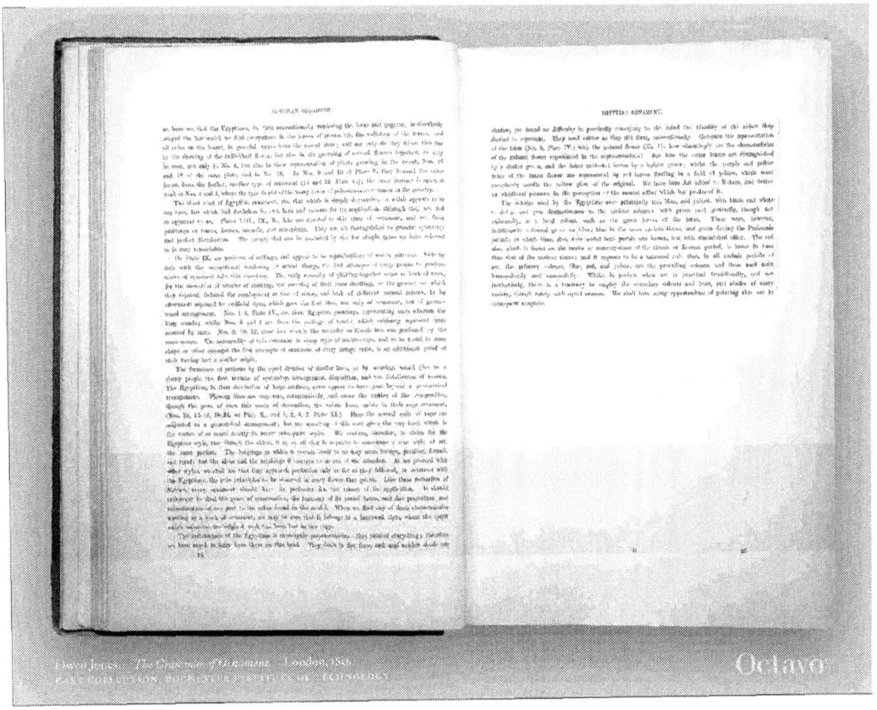
The Grammar of Ornament. London, 1856.
Octavo

Owen Jones. The Grammar of Ornament. London, 1856.

EGYPTIAN Nº 2.

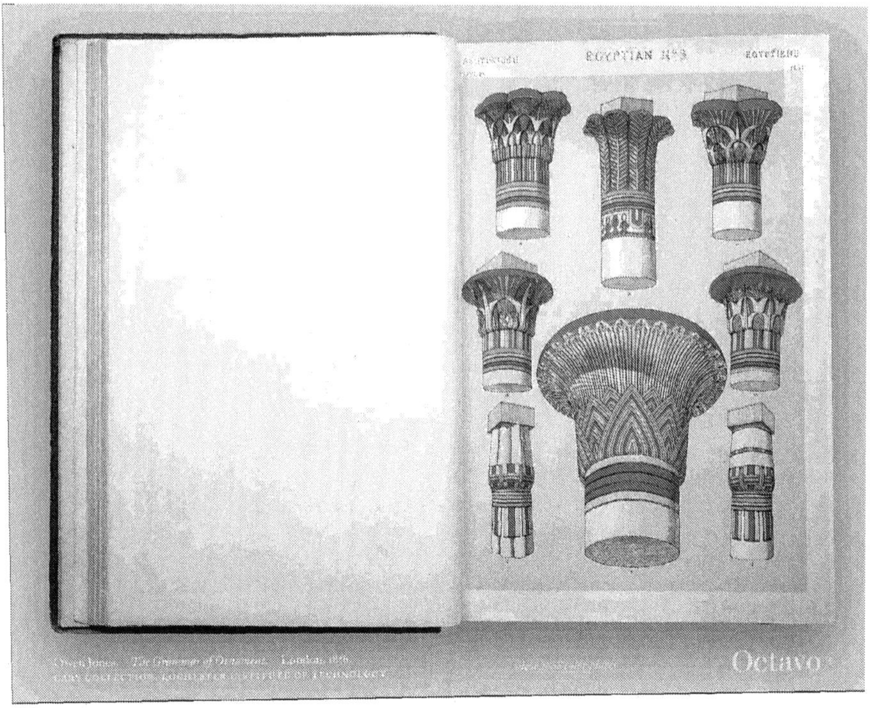
EGYPTIAN No 3
Owen Jones. The Grammar of Ornament. London, 1856.
GARY COLLECTION, ROCHESTER INSTITUTE OF TECHNOLOGY
Octavo

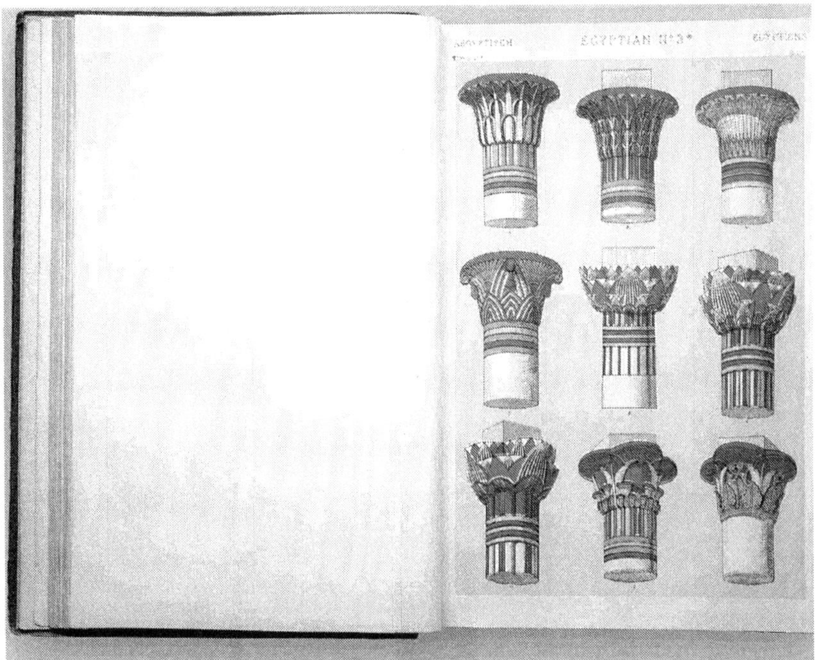

Owen Jones. *The Grammar of Ornament*. London, 1856.

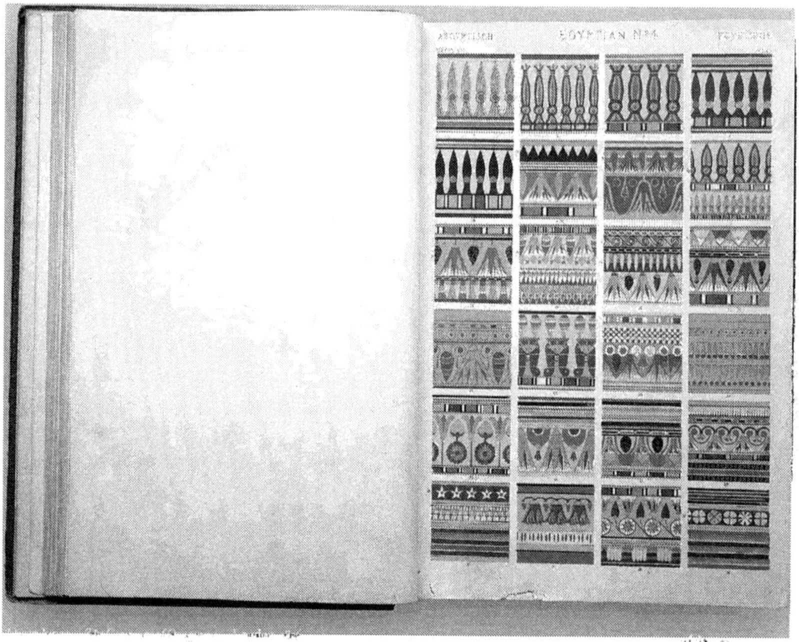
EGYPTIAN No 4

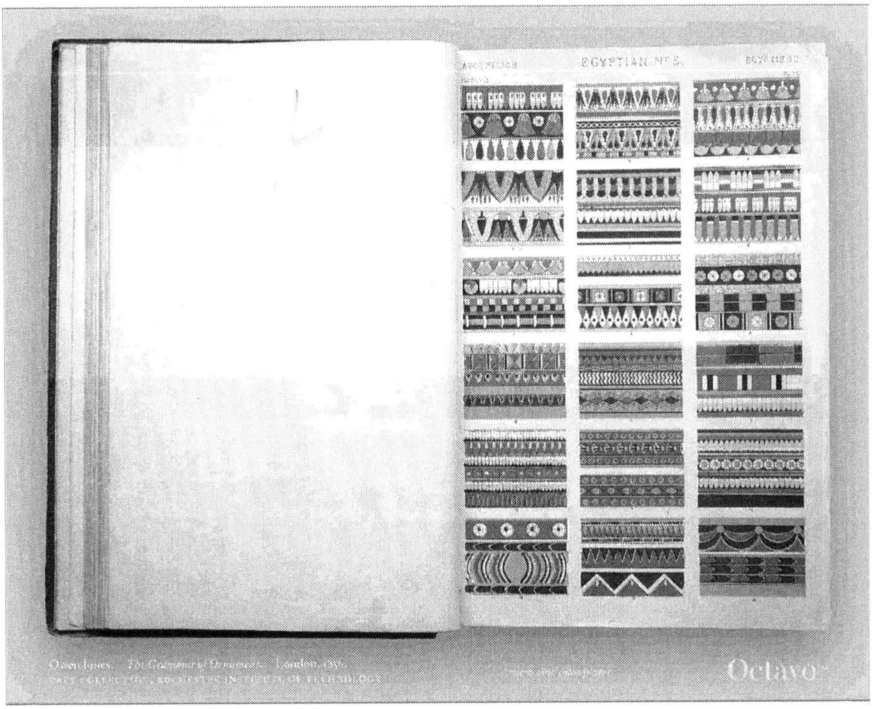
EGYPTIAN Nº 5.
Owen Jones. The Grammar of Ornament. London, 1856.
Octavo

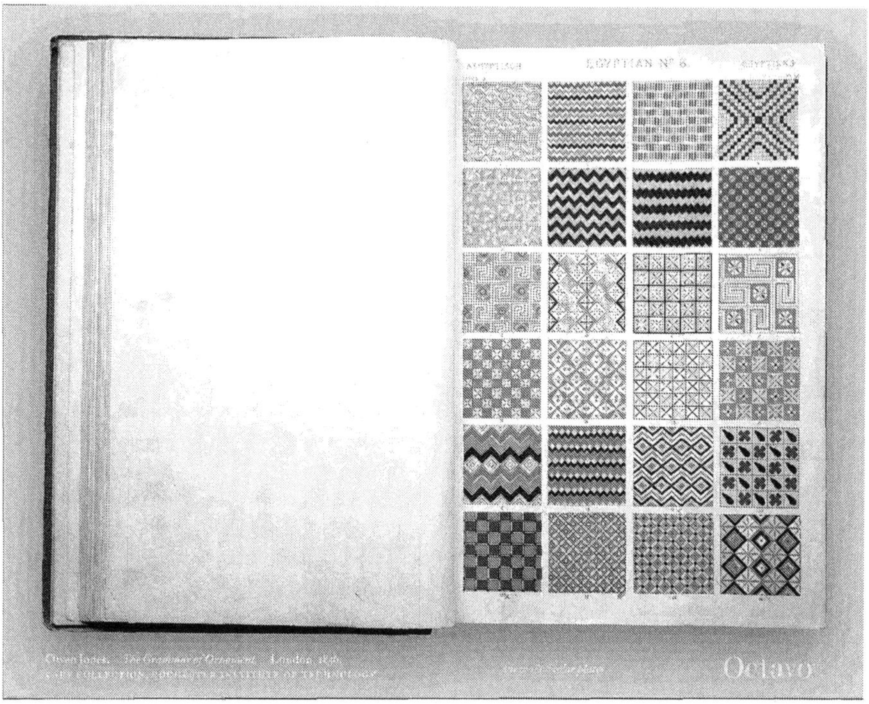
EGYPTIAN Nº 6.
Octavo

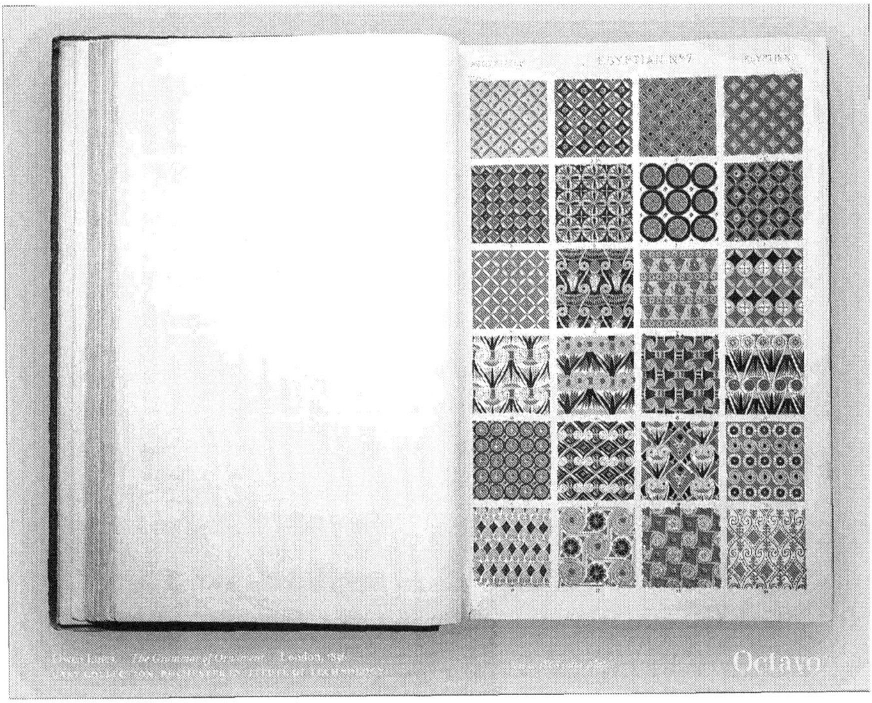
EGYPTIAN Nº 7
Octavo

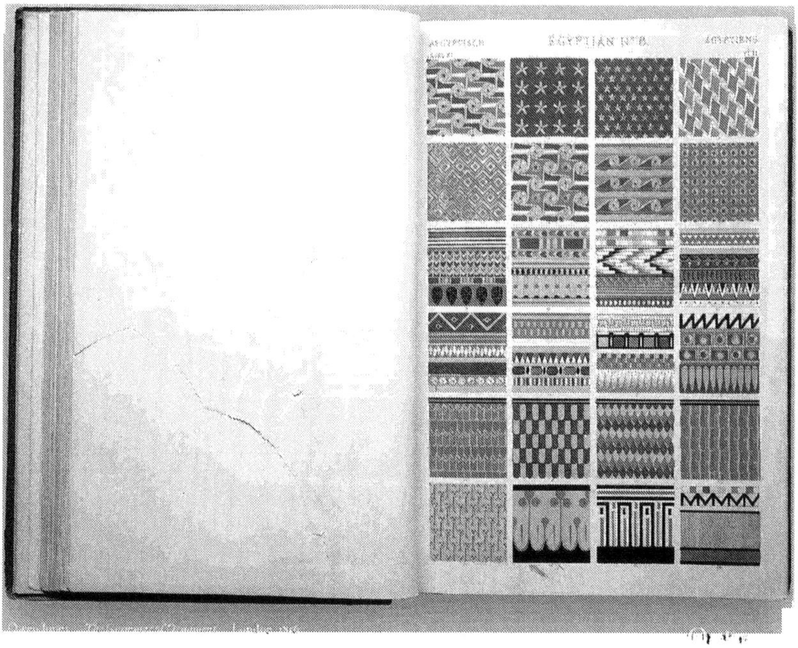
EGYPTIAN Nº 8.

CHAPTER III. PLATES 12, 13, 14.

ASSYRIAN AND PERSIAN ORNAMENT.

PLATE XII.

[illegible]

[illegible]

PLATE XIII.

[illegible]

[illegible]

PLATE XIV.

[illegible]

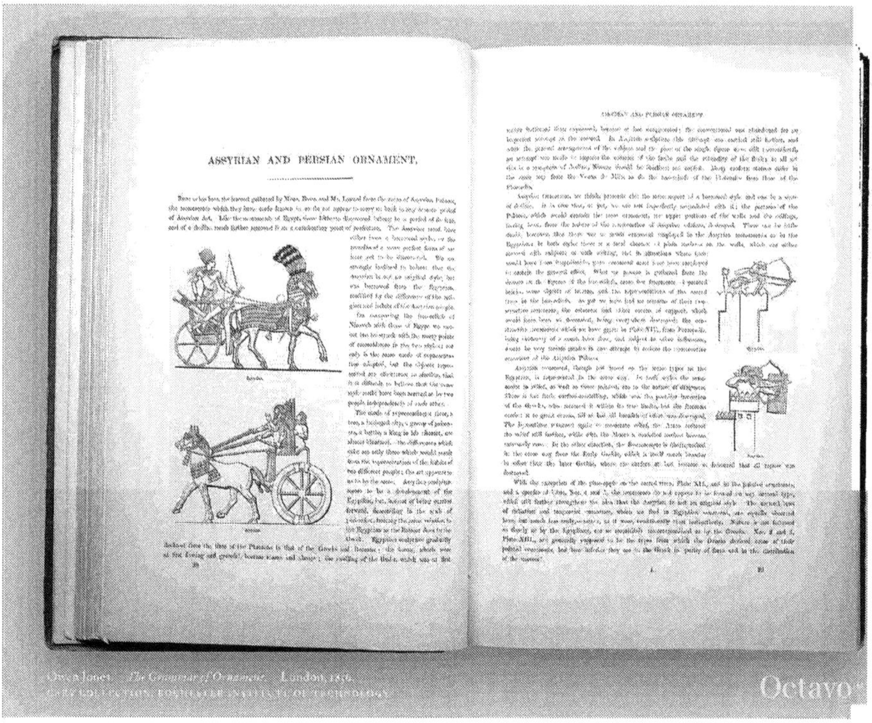

ASSYRIAN AND PERSIAN ORNAMENT.

Owen Jones. *The Grammar of Ornament.* London, 1856.
CARY COLLECTION, ROCHESTER INSTITUTE OF TECHNOLOGY

The colours in use by the Assyrians appear to have been blue, red, white, and black, on their painted ornaments; blue, red, and gold, on their sculptured ornaments; and green, orange, buff, white and black, on their enamelled bricks.

The ornaments of *Persepolis*, represented on Plate XIV., appear to be modifications of Roman details. Nos. 3, 5, 6, 7, 8, are from bases of fluted columns, which evidently betray a Roman influence. The ornaments from Tak I Bostan,—17, 20, 21, 23, 24,—are all constructed on the same principle as Roman ornament, presenting only a similar modification of the modelled surface, such as we find in Byzantine ornament, and which they resemble in a most remarkable manner.

The ornaments, 18 and 19, from *Sassanian* capitals, Byzantine in their general outline, at Bi Sutoun, contain the germs of all the ornamentation of the Arabs and Moors. It is the earliest example we meet with of lozenge-shaped diapers. The Egyptians and the Assyrians appear to have covered large spaces with patterns formed by geometrical arrangement of lines, but this is the first instance of the repetition of curved lines forming a general pattern enclosing a secondary form. By the principle contained in No. 18 would be generated all those exquisite forms of diaper which covered the domes of the mosques of Cairo and the walls of the Alhambra.

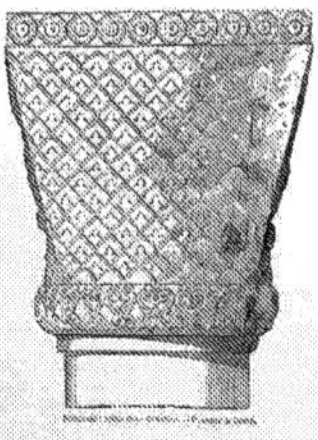

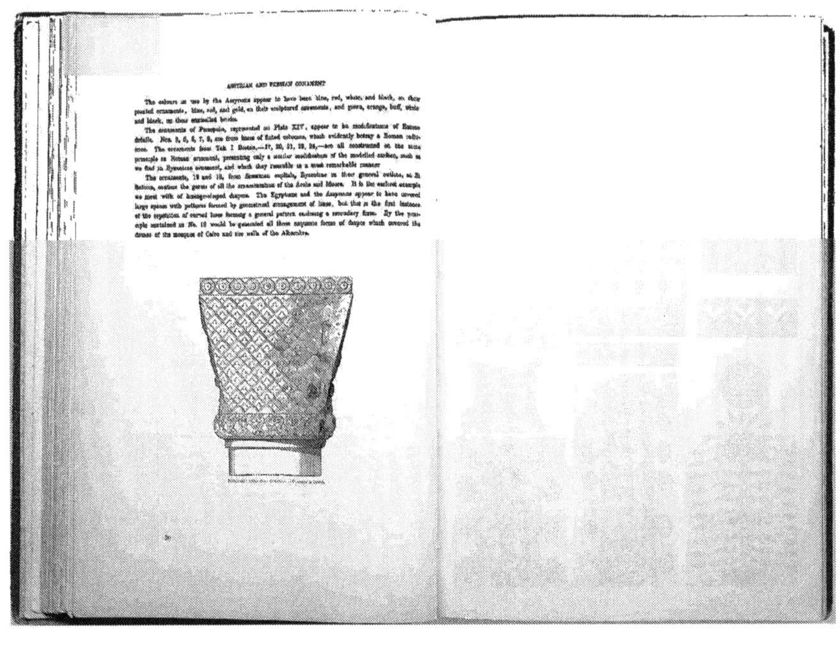

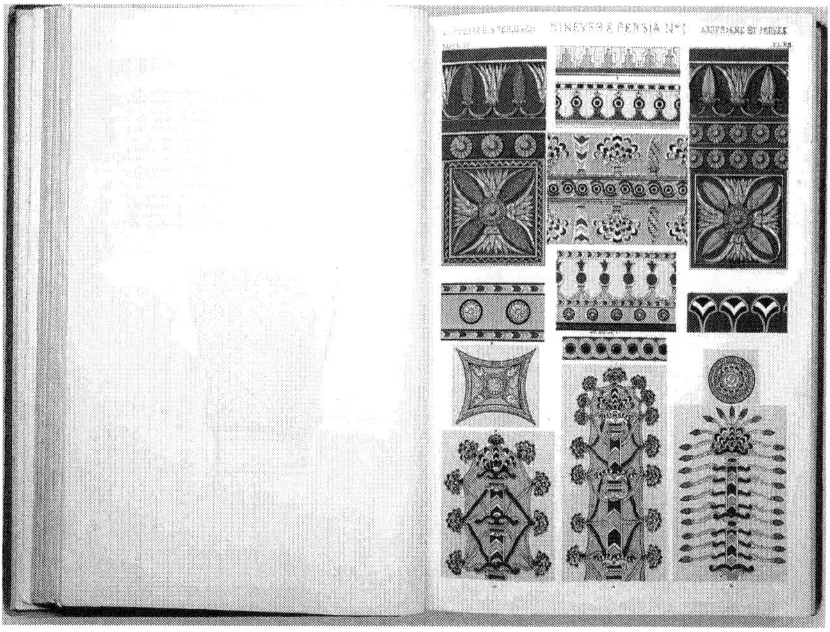
NINEVEH & PERSIA N° 1

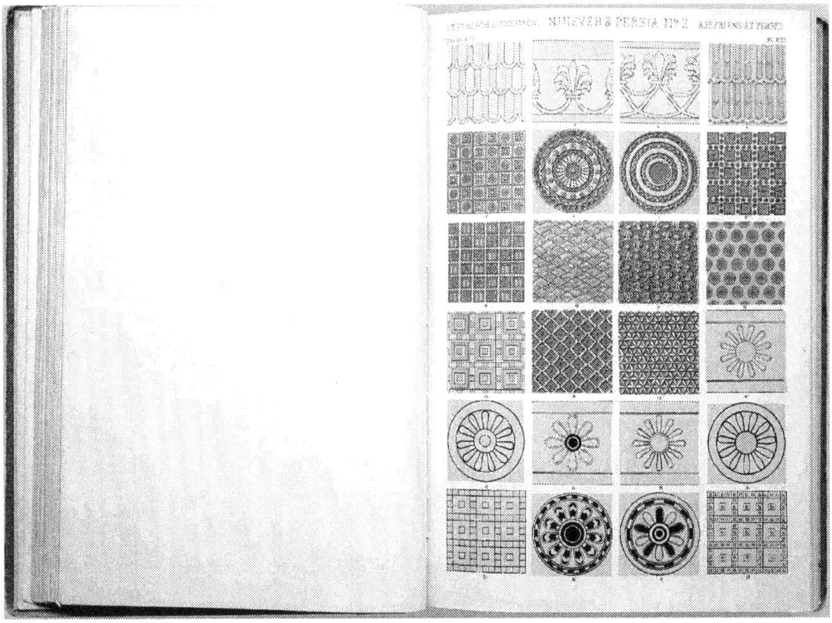
NINEVEH & PERSIA No 2
ASSYRIENS ET PERSES

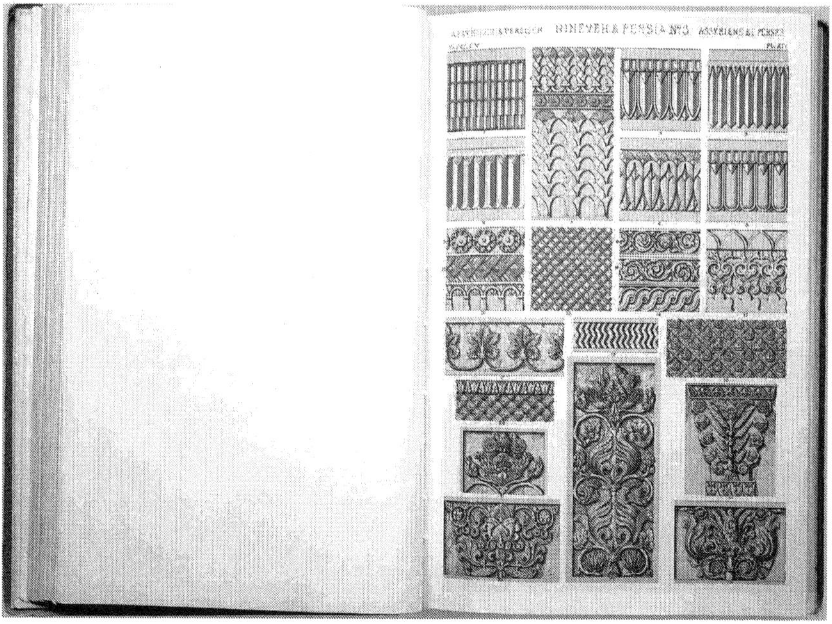
NINEVEH & PERSIA No 3.

Chapter IV. Plates 15, 16, 17, 18, 19, 20, 21, 22.

GREEK ORNAMENT.

PLATE XV.

A collection of the various forms of the Greek Fret from Vases and Pavements.

PLATE XVI.–XXI.

Ornaments from Greek and Etruscan Vases in the British Museum and the Louvre.

PLATE XXII.

1 and 4. From a Sarcophagus, in Sicily.—Hittorff.
[illegible]. From the Propylæa, Athens.—Hittorff.
[illegible]. From the Cornice of the Ceiling of the Propylæa.—Penrose.
13. [illegible] Published by Mr. Penrose in gold only; we have supplied the blue and red.
[illegible]. Painted Ornaments.—Hittorff.
22 and 27. Ornaments in Terra Cotta.
28. Painted Ornament from the Cymatium of Crowning Cornice of the Parthenon.—L. Vulliamy. The blue and red supplied.
[illegible]. Various Frets, the traces of which exist on all the Temples at Athens. The colours supplied.

We have seen that Egyptian Ornament was derived direct from natural inspiration, that it was founded on a few types, and that it remained unchanged during the whole course of Egyptian civilisation, except in the more or less perfection of the execution, the more ancient monuments being the most perfect. We have further expressed our belief that the Assyrian was a borrowed style, possessing none of the characteristics of original inspiration, but rather appearing to have been suggested by the Art of Egypt, already in its decline, which decline was carried still further. Greek Art, on the contrary, though borrowed partly from the Egyptian and partly from the Assyrian, was the development of an old idea in a new direction; and, unrestrained by religious laws, as would appear to have been both the Assyrian and the Egyptian, Greek Art rose rapidly to a high state of perfection, from which it was itself able to give forth the elements of future greatness to other styles. It carried

[illegible]

[illegible]

[illegible]

the perfection of pure form to a point which has never since been reached; and from the very abundant remains we have of Greek ornament, we must believe the presence of refined taste was

almost universal, and that the land was overflowing with artists, whose hands and minds were so trained as to enable them to execute these beautiful ornaments with unerring truth.

Greek ornament was wanting, however, in one of the great charms which should always accompany ornament,—viz. Symbolism. It was meaningless, purely decorative, never representative, and can hardly be said to be constructive, for the various members of a Greek monument rather present surfaces exquisitely designed to receive ornament, which they did, at first, painted, and in later times both carved and painted. The ornament was no part of the construction, as with the Egyptian: it could be removed, and the structure remained unchanged. On the Corinthian capital the ornament is applied, not constructed: it is not so on the Egyptian capital; there we feel the whole capital is the ornament,—to remove any portion of it would destroy it.

However much we admire the extreme and almost divine perfection of the Greek monumental sculpture, in its application the Greeks frequently went beyond the legitimate bounds of ornament. The frieze of the Parthenon was placed so far from the eye that it became a diagram: the beauties which so astonish us when seen near the eye could only have been valuable so far as they evidenced the artist-worship which cared not that the eye saw the perfection of the work if conscious that it was to be found there; but we are bound to consider this an abuse of means, and that the Greeks were in this respect inferior to the Egyptians, whose system of intaglio relievo for monumental sculpture appears to us the more perfect.

The examples of representative ornament are very few, with the exception of the wave ornament and the fret used to distinguish water from land in their pictures, and some conventional renderings of trees, as at No. 12, Plate XXI., we have little that can deserve that appellation; but of decorative ornament the Greek and Etruscan vases supply us with abundant materials, and as the painted ornaments of the Temples, which have as yet been discovered in no way differ from them, we have little doubt that we are acquainted with Greek ornament in all its phases. Like the Egyptian the types are few, but the conventional rendering is much further removed from the types. In the well-known honeysuckle ornament it is difficult to recognise any attempt at imitation, but rather an appreciation of the principle on which the flower grows, and, indeed, on examining the paintings on the vases, we are rather tempted to believe that the various forms of the leaves of a Greek flower have been generated by the brush of the painter, according as the hand is turned upwards or downwards in the formation of the leaf would the character be given, and it is more likely that the slight resemblance to the honeysuckle may have been an after recognition than that the natural flower should have ever served as the model. In Plate XCIX. will be found a representation of the honeysuckle, and how faint indeed is the resemblance. What is evident is, that the Greeks in their ornament were close observers of nature, and although they did not copy, or attempt to imitate, they worked on the same principles. The three great laws which we find everywhere in nature—radiation from the parent stem, proportionate distribution of the areas, and the tangential curvature of the lines—are always obeyed, and it is the unerring perfection with which they are, in the most humble works as in the highest, which excites our astonishment, and which is only fully realised on attempting to reproduce Greek ornament, so rarely done with success. A very characteristic feature of Greek ornament, continued by the Romans, but abandoned during the Byzantine period, is, that the various parts of a scroll grow out of each other in a continuous line, as the ornament from the Choragic Monument of Lysicrates.

In the Byzantine, the Arabian, Moresque, and Early English styles, the flowers flow off on either side from a continuous line. We have here an instance how slight a change in any

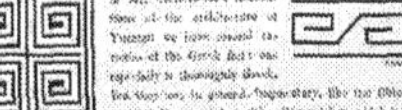

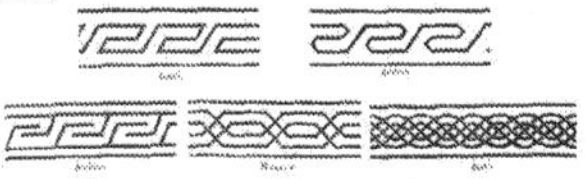

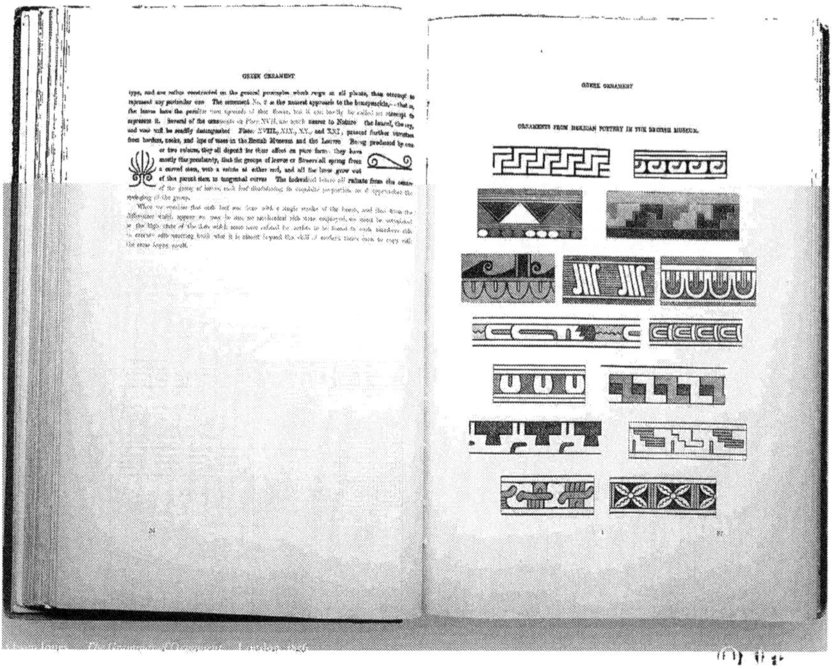
GREEK ORNAMENT
GREEK ORNAMENT
ORNAMENTS FROM MEXICAN POTTERY IN THE BRITISH MUSEUM.

GREEK No 1
Owen Jones. The Grammar of Ornament. London, 1856.
Octavo

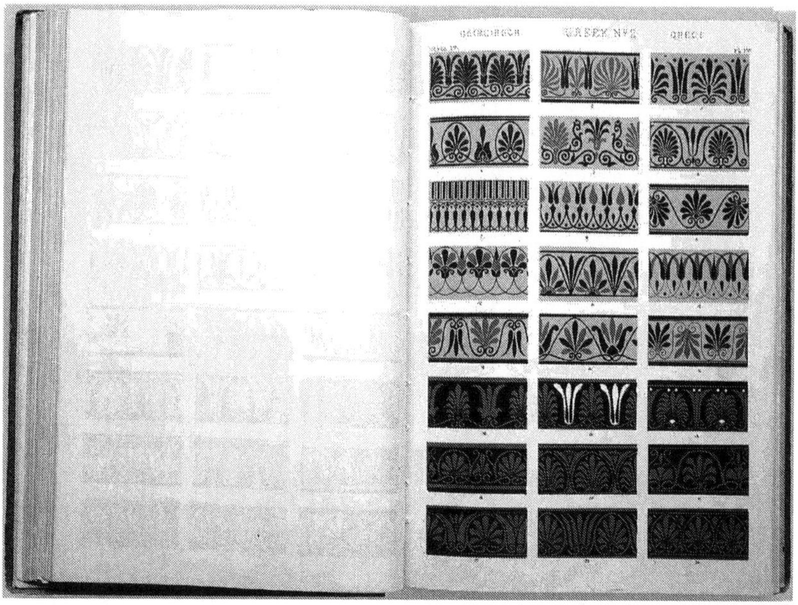
GREEK Nº2

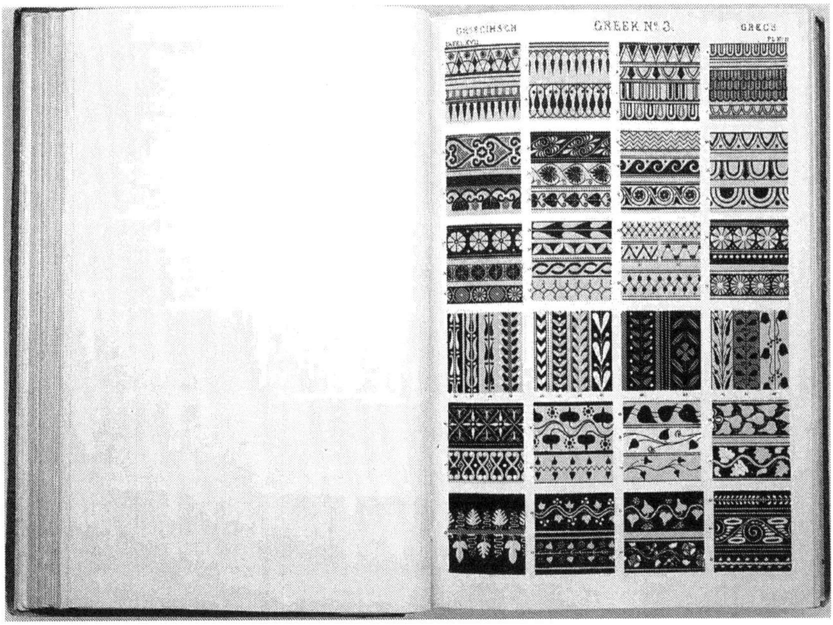
GREEK Nº 3.
GREC

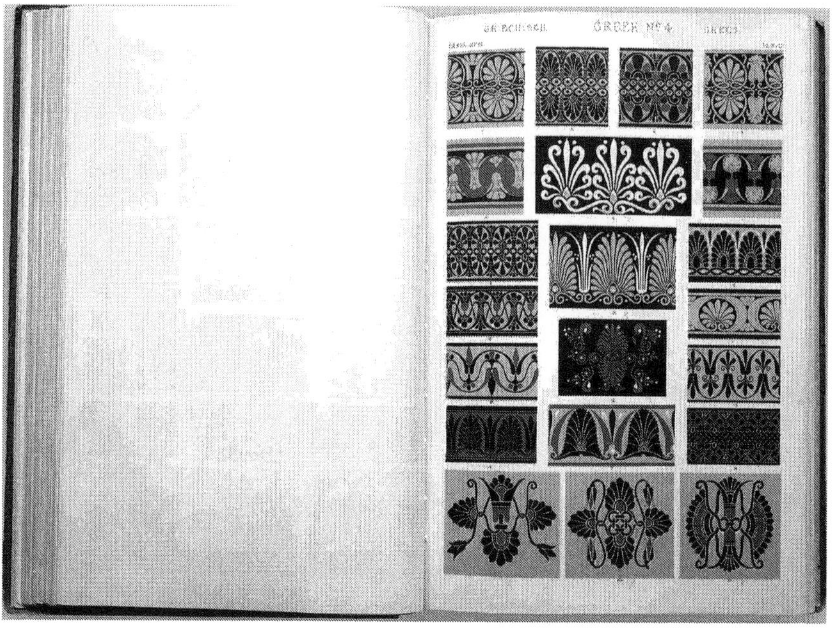
GRIECHISCH. GREEK Nº4 GRECS

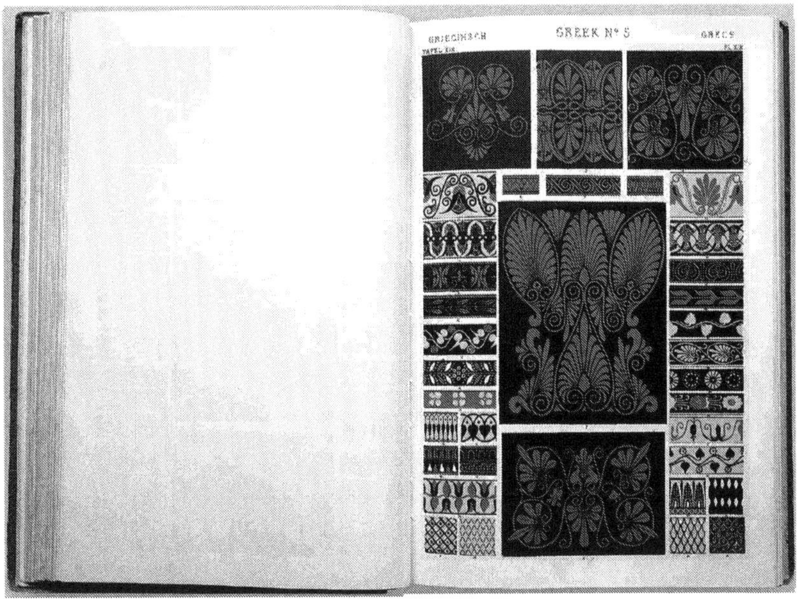
GRIECHISCH
GREEK Nº 5

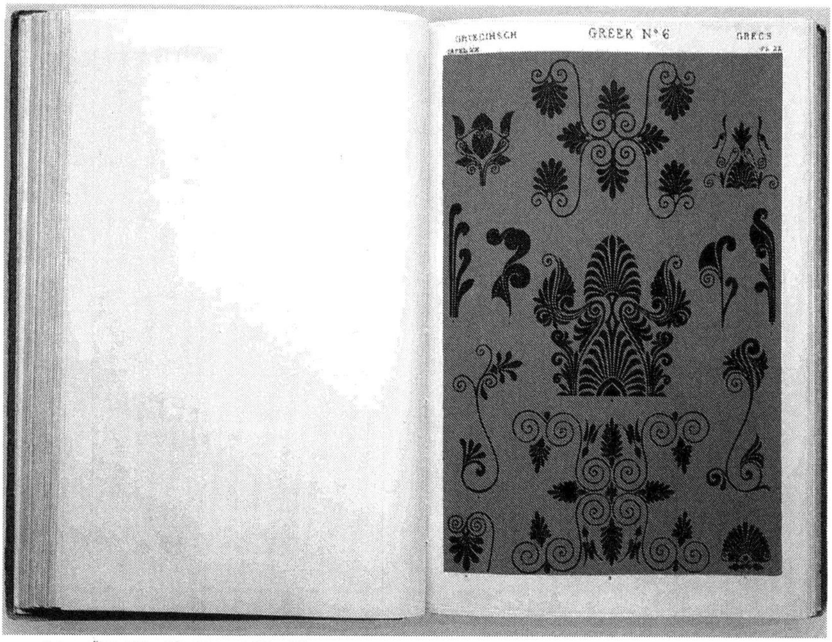
GRIECHISCH
GREEK N° 6
GRECS

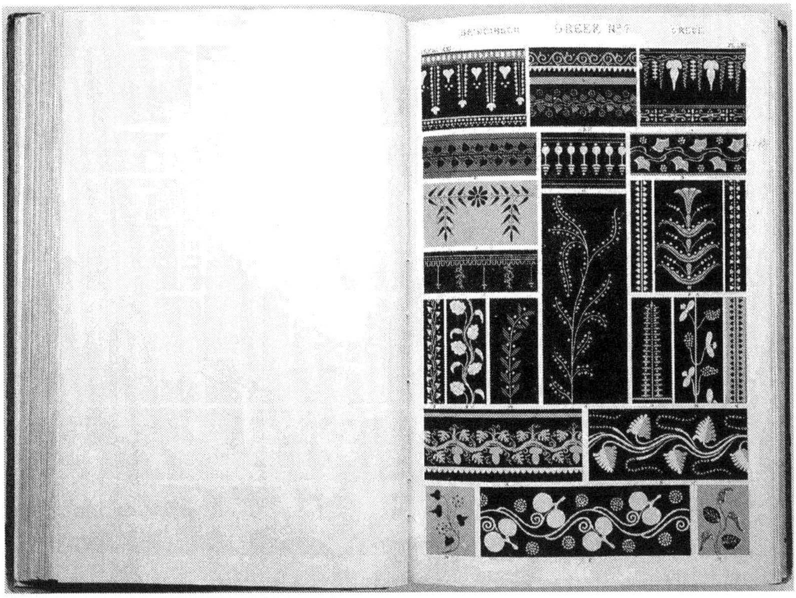
GREEK Nº 7

GREEK No 8

Chapter V.—Plates 23, 24, 25.

POMPEIAN ORNAMENT.

PLATE XXIII.

Collection of Borders from different Houses in Pompeii.—Zahn's Pompeii.

PLATE XXIV.

Various Pilasters and Friezes from different Houses in Pompeii.—Zahn's Pompeii.

PLATE XXV.

Collection of Mosaics from Pompeii and the Museum at Naples.—From the Author's Sketches.

The ornament of Pompeii has been so ably and so fully illustrated in Zahn's magnificent work, that we have thought it only necessary for this series to borrow from him the materials for two plates, to illustrate the two distinct styles of ornament which prevail in the decorations of the edifices of Pompeii. The first (Plate XXIII.) are evidently of Greek origin, composed of conventional ornaments in flat tints, either painted dark on a light ground, or light on a dark ground, but without shade or any attempt at relief; the second (Plate XXIV.) are more Roman in character, based upon the acanthus scroll, and interwoven with ornament in direct imitation of Nature.

We refer the reader to Zahn's work* for a full appreciation of the system of ornamentation in use at Pompeii. An examination of this work will show that this system was carried to the very limits of caprice, and that almost any theory of colouring and decoration could be supported by authority from Pompeii.

The general arrangement of the decoration on the walls of the interior of a Pompeian house

* Les plus beaux Ornemens et les Tableaux les plus Remarquables de Pompéi, d'Herculanum, et de Stabiæ, &c., par Guillaume Zahn. Berlin, 1828.

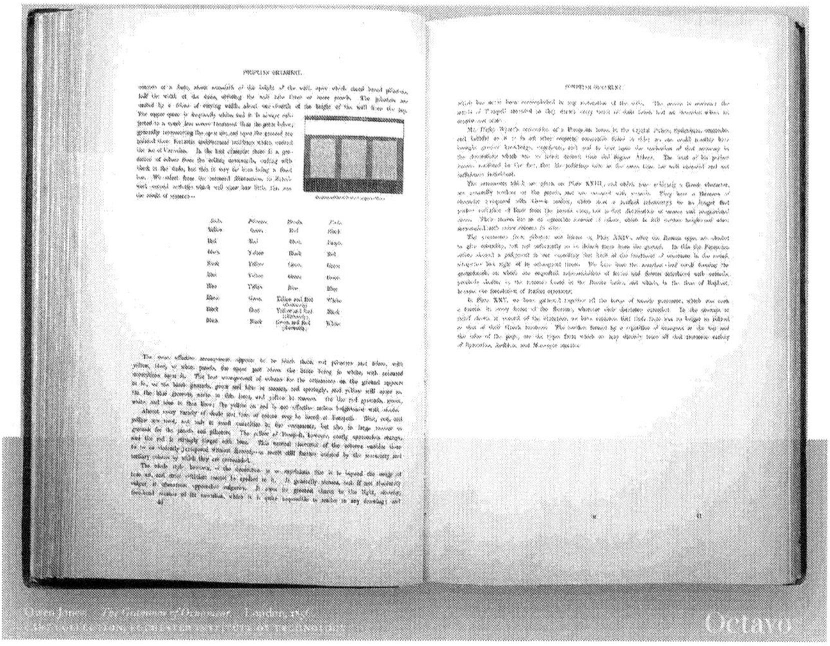
Owen Jones The Grammar of Ornament London, 1856
CARY COLLECTION, ROCHESTER INSTITUTE OF TECHNOLOGY
Octavo

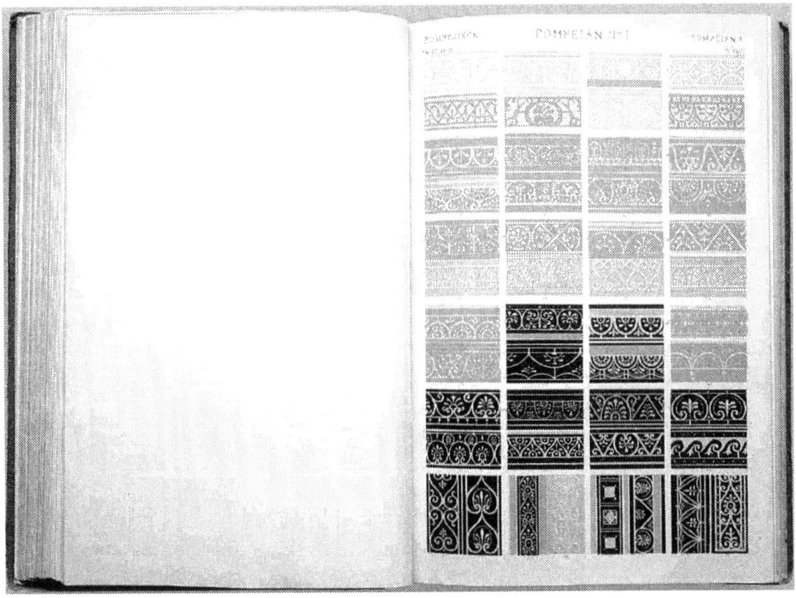
POMPEIAN No 1

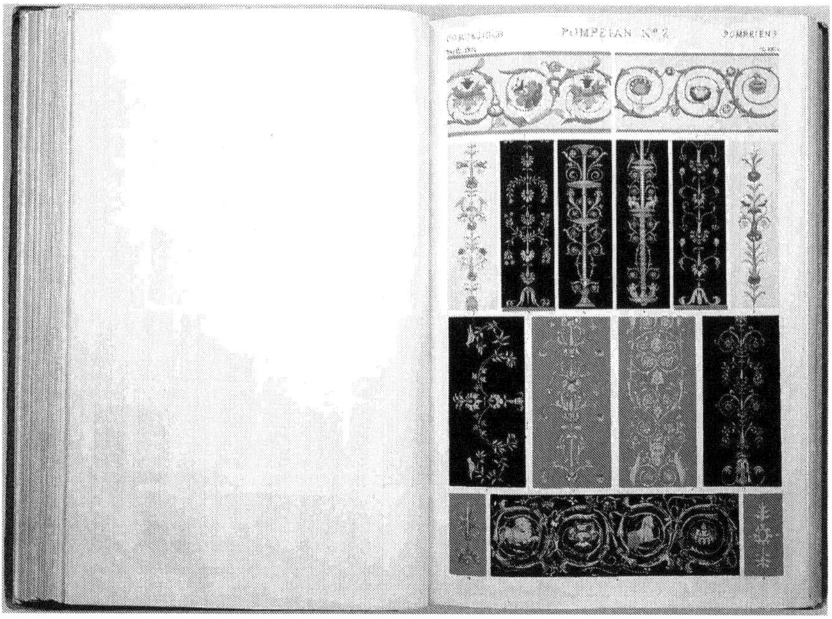
POMPEIAN Nº 2.

POMPEIAN No 3

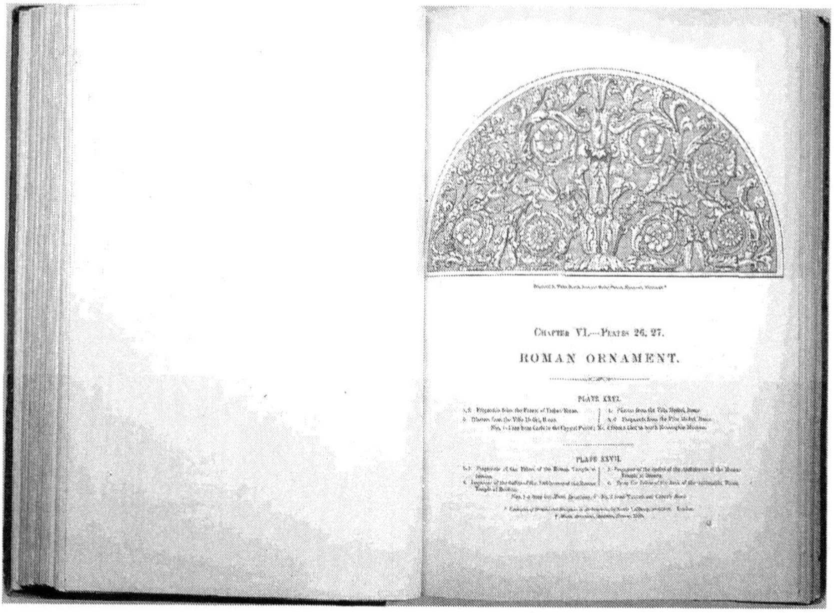

CHAPTER VI.—PLATES 26, 27.
ROMAN ORNAMENT.
PLATE XXVI.
PLATE XXVII.

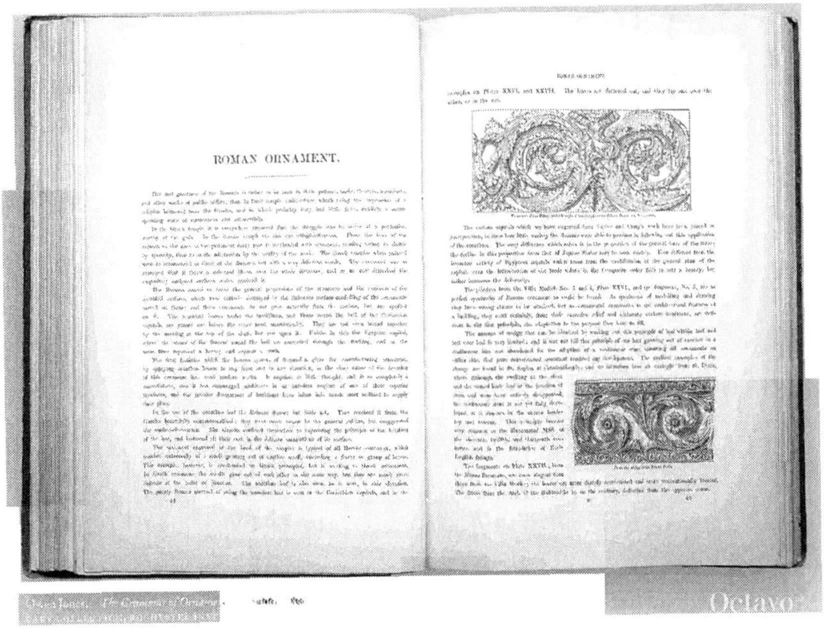

Owen Jones. The Grammar of Ornament.

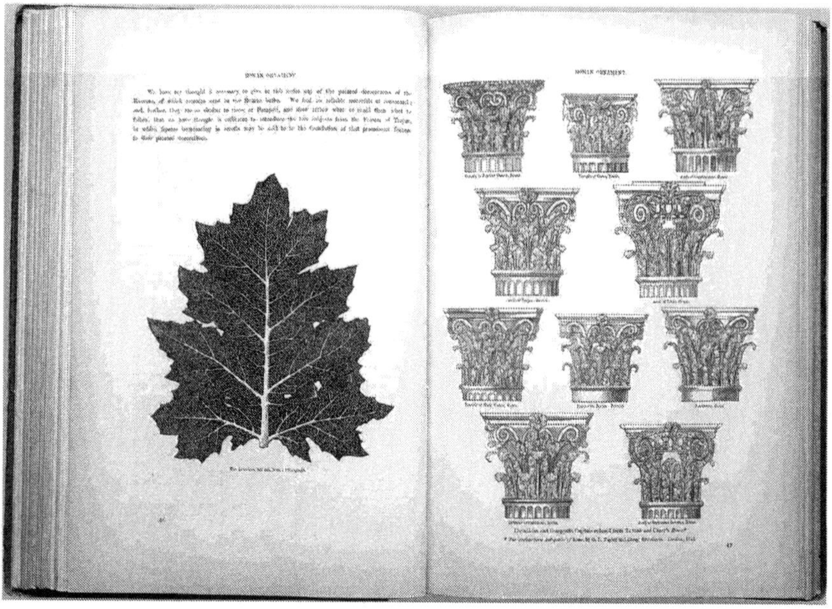

ROMAN No 1
ROMAINS.

ROMAN Nº 2

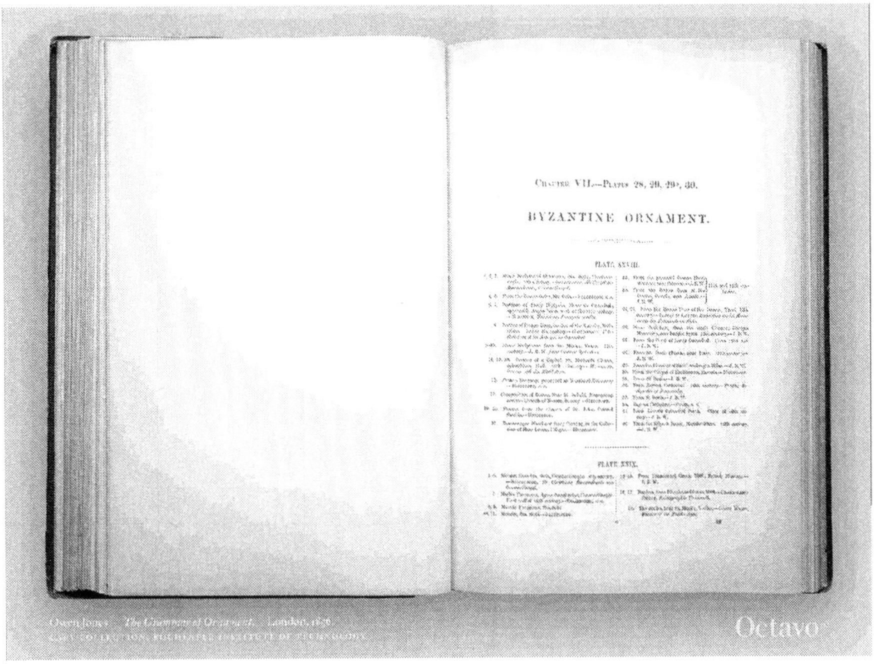
CHAPTER VII.—PLATES 28, 29, 29*, 30.
BYZANTINE ORNAMENT.
PLATE XXVIII.
PLATE XXIX.
Octavo

PLATE XXIX.

PLATE XXX.

BYZANTINE ORNAMENT.

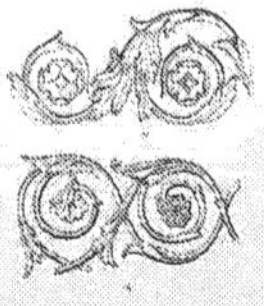

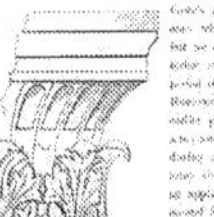

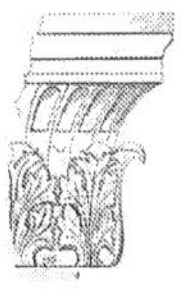

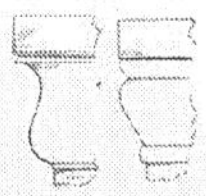

J. B. WARING.

BOOKS REFERRED TO FOR ILLUSTRATIONS.

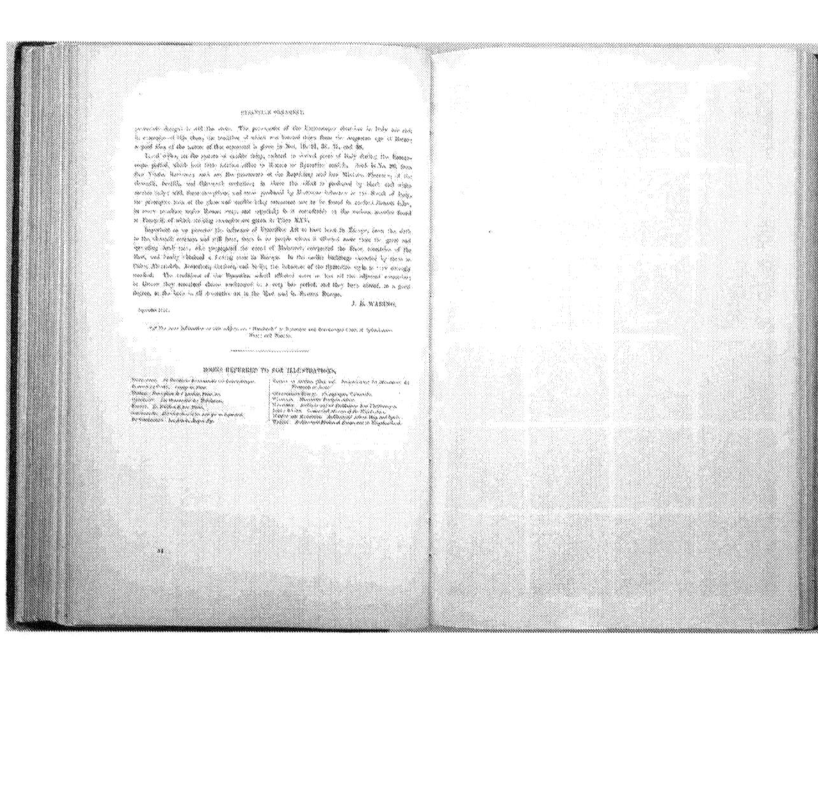

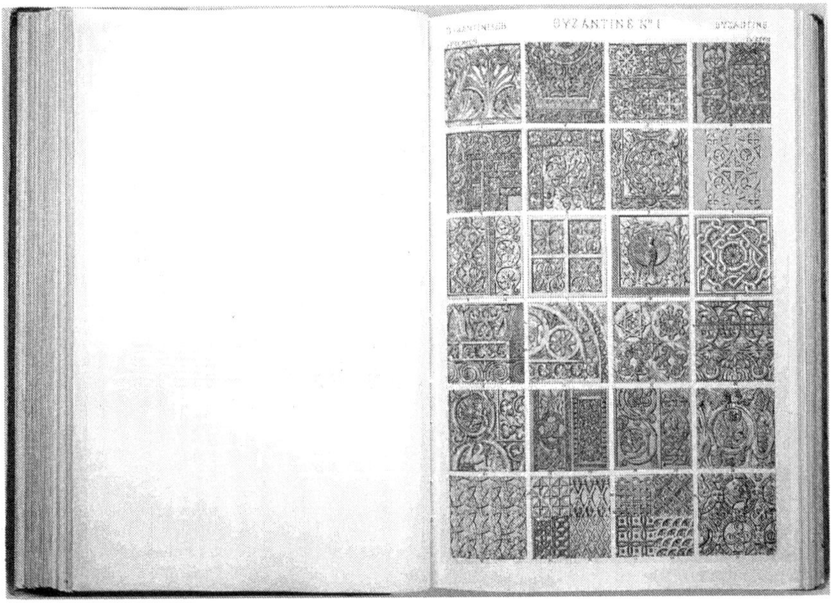
BYZANTINE No. 1

BYZANTINE No 2

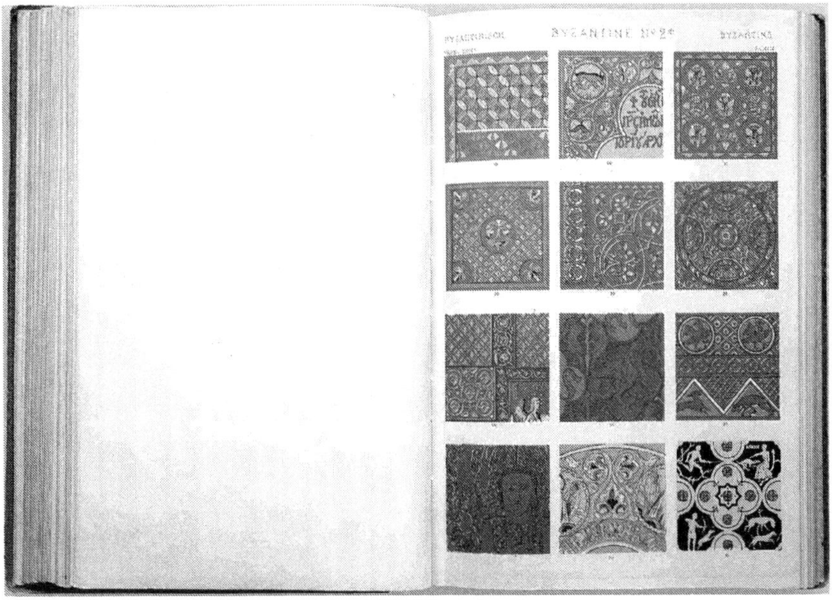
BYZANTINE

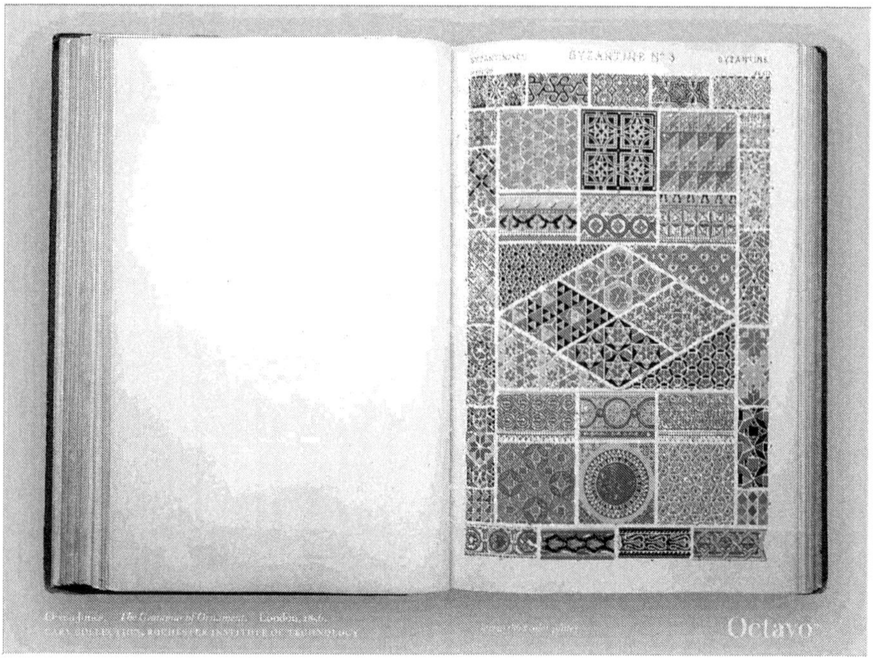
BYZANTINE Nº 3
Octavo

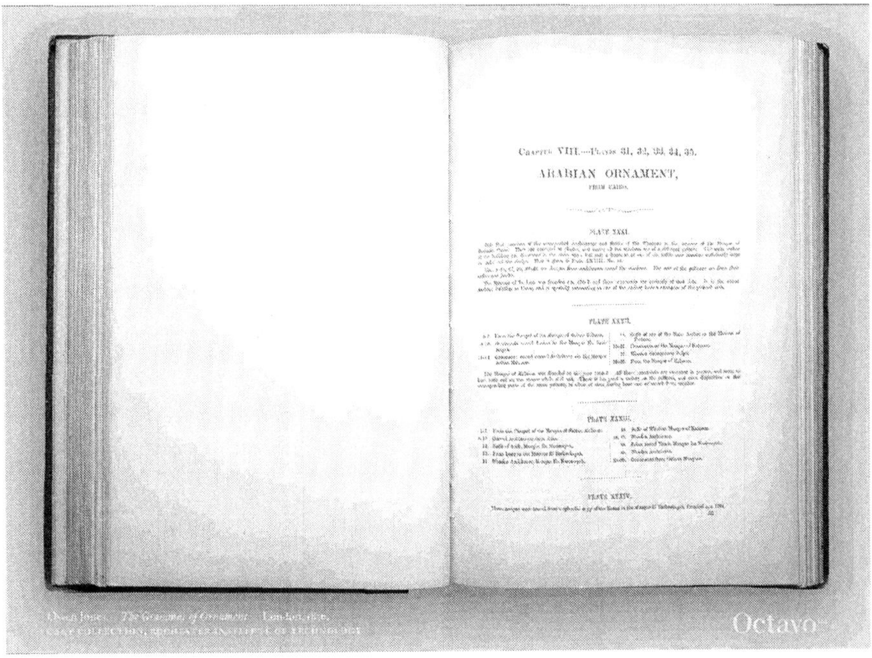
ARABIAN ORNAMENT,
Octavo

PLATE XXXV.

[illegible]

ARABIAN ORNAMENT.

[illegible]

[illegible]

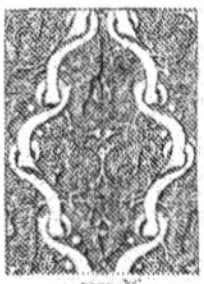

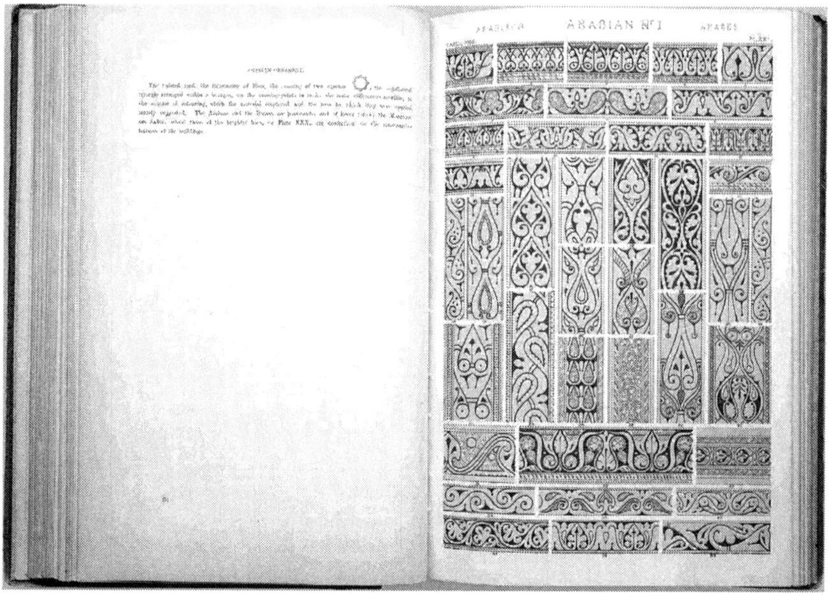
ARABIAN Nº 1

ARABIAN Nº2

ARABIAN Nº 3

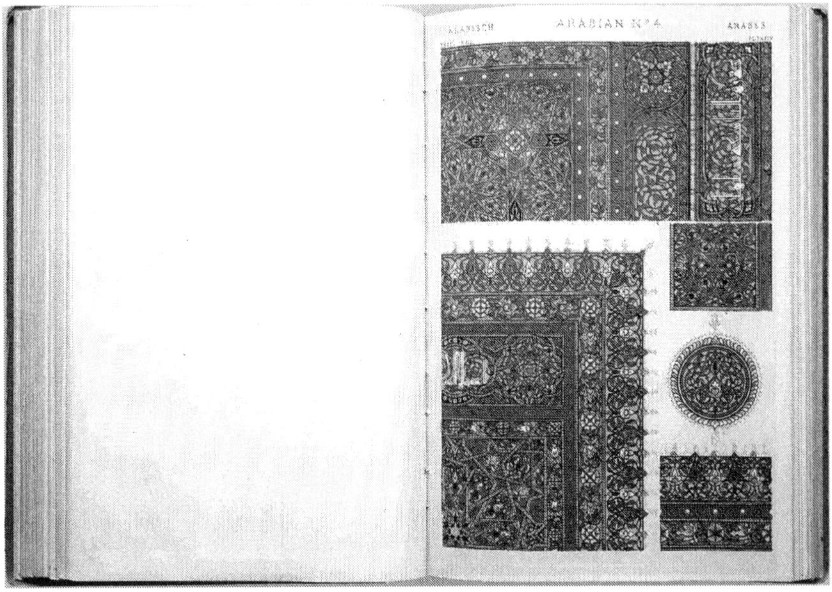
ARABIAN Nº 4

ARABISCH
ARABIAN
ARABES

Chapter IX.—Plates 36, 37, 38.

TURKISH ORNAMENT.

PLATE XXXVI.

1, 2, 3, 13, 15. From a Fountain at [illegible], Constantinople.
4. From the Mosque of Sultan Achmet, Constantinople.
5, 6, 7, 9, 12. From Tombs at Constantinople.
8, 10, 11, 12. From the Tomb of Soliman I., Constantinople.
16, 17, 18, 19, 21. From the Yeni Djami, Constantinople.
20, 22. From a Fountain at [illegible], Constantinople.

PLATE XXXVII.

1, 2, 3, 5, 6. From the Yeni Djami, Constantinople.
4. Border in the Centre of the Dome of the Mosque of Soliman I., Constantinople.
7, 8. [illegible] the Dome of the Mosque of Soliman I., Constantinople.

PLATE XXXVIII.

Portion of the Decoration of the Dome of the Tomb of Soliman I., Constantinople.

The architecture of the Turks, as seen at Constantinople, is in all its structural features wholly based upon the early Byzantine monuments: their system of ornamentation, however, is a modification of the Arabian, bearing about the same relation to it as the Elizabethan ornament does to Italian Renaissance.

When the art of one people is adopted by another having the same religion, but differing in natural character and instincts, we should expect to find a deficiency in all those qualities in which the borrowing people are inferior to their predecessors. And thus it is with the art of the Turks as compared with the art of the Arabs; there is the same difference in the amount of elegance and refinement in the art of the two people as exists in their national character.

We are, however, inclined to believe that the Turks have rarely themselves practised the arts, but that they have rather commissioned their execution than been themselves executants. All their mosques and public buildings present a mixed style. On the same building, side by side with ornaments derived from Arabian and Persian floral ornaments, we find debased Roman and Renaissance details, leading to the belief that these buildings have mostly been executed by artists differing in religion from themselves. In [illegible] the Turks [illegible]

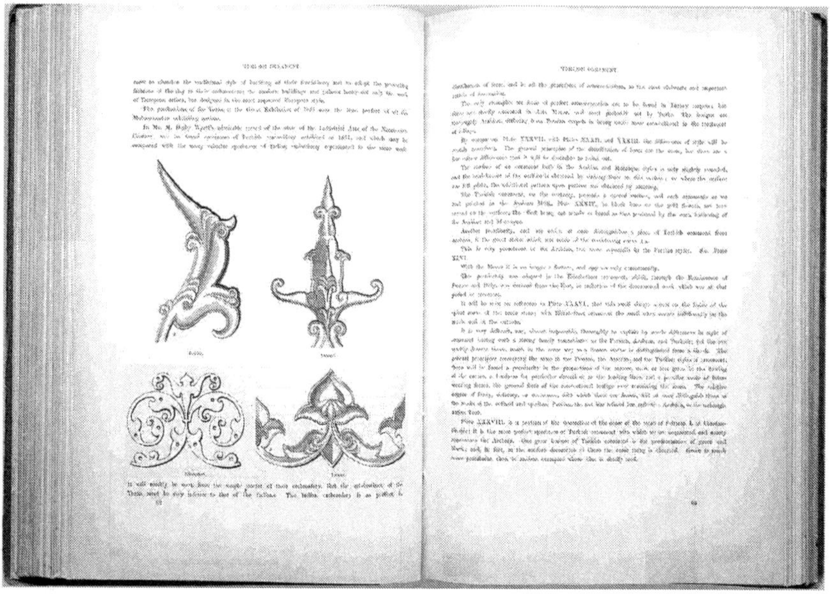

TURKISH N° 1
London, 1856.
Octavo

TURKISH No 2
Owen Jones. The Grammar of Ornament. London 1856.
Octavo

Owen Jones
The Grammar of Ornament
London, 1856
Octavo

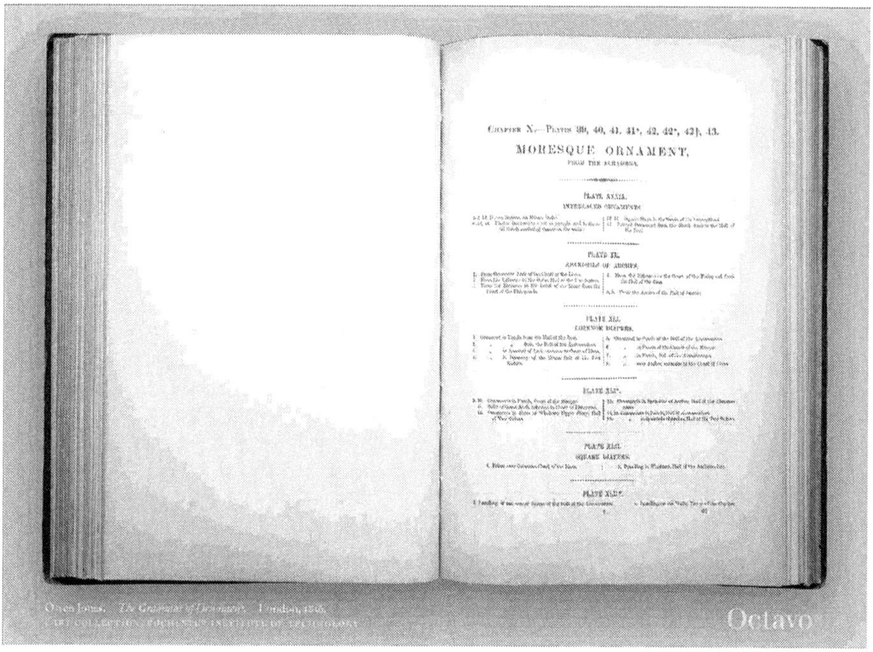
MORESQUE ORNAMENT,
Octavo

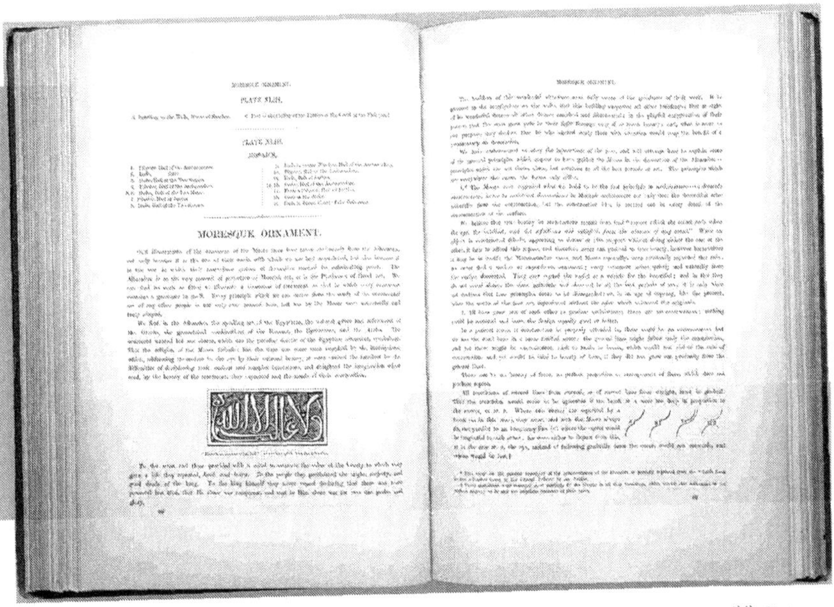
MORESQUE ORNAMENT.

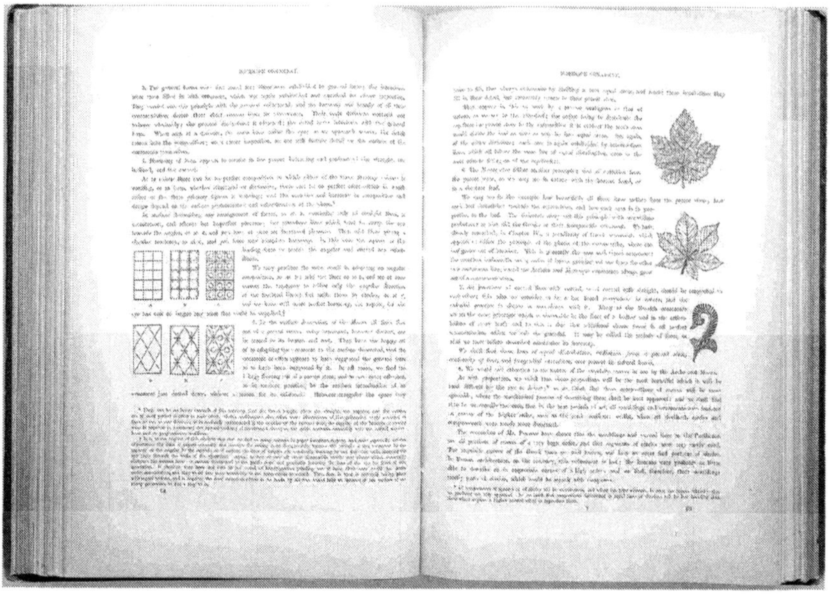

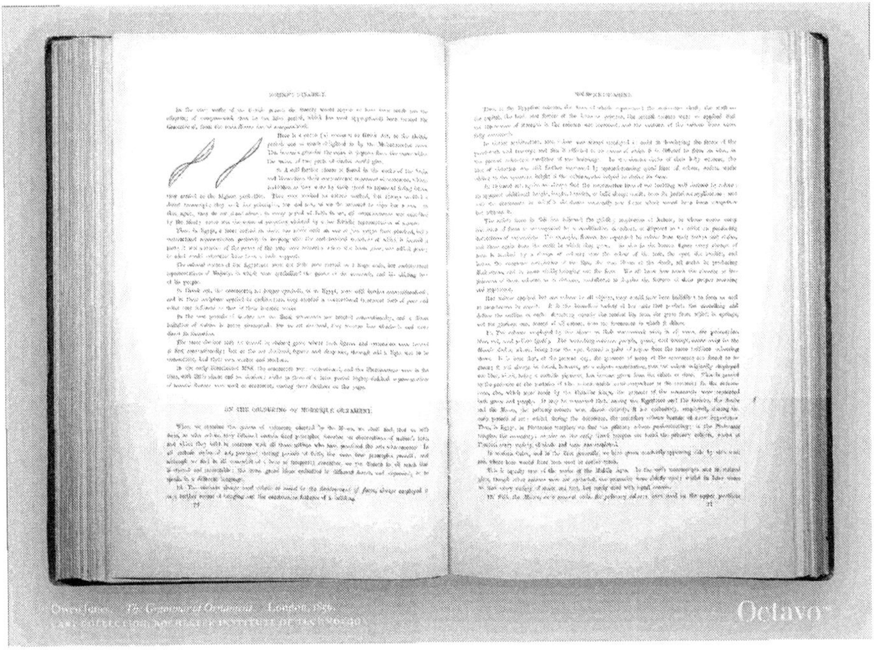
Owen Jones. The Grammar of Ornament. London, 1856.
Octavo

INTERLACED PATTERNS

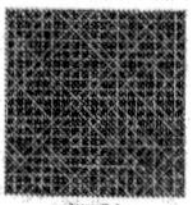

LOZENGE DIAPERS

SQUARE DIAPERS

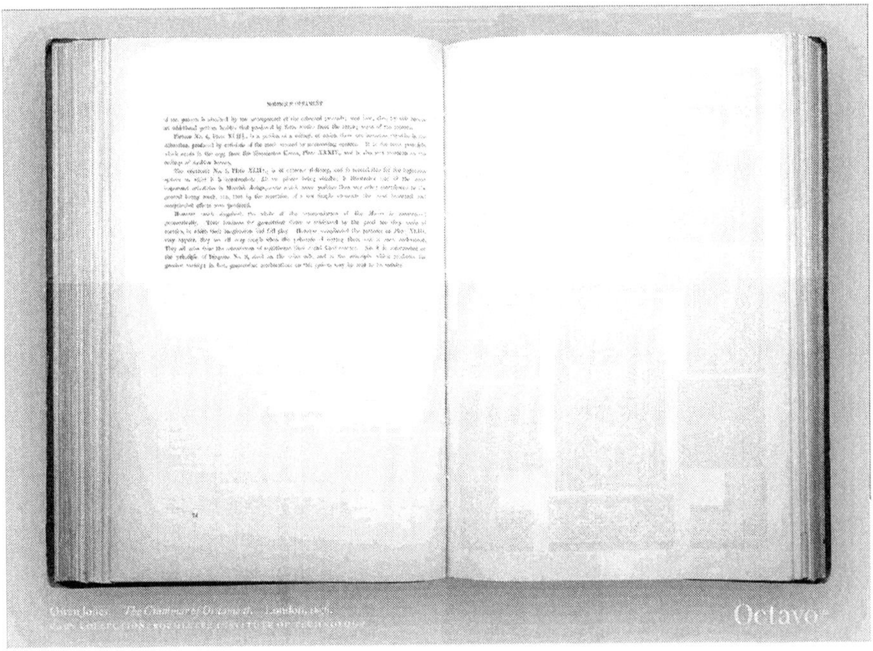
Owen Jones *The Grammar of Ornament.* London
Octavo

Octavo

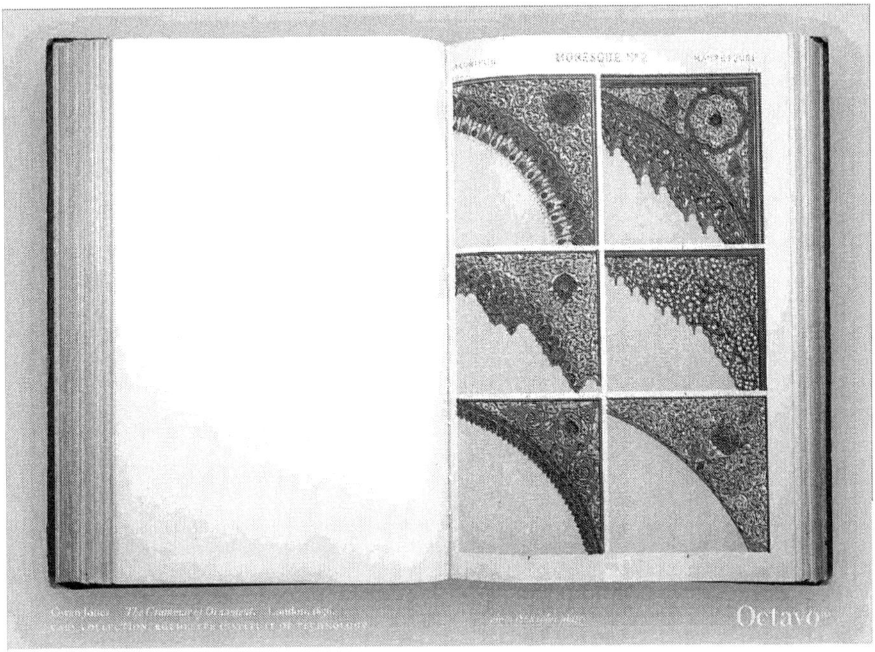
MORESQUE Nº 2
Octavo

MORESQUE No 3
Owen Jones. The Grammar of Ornament. London, 1856.
Octavo

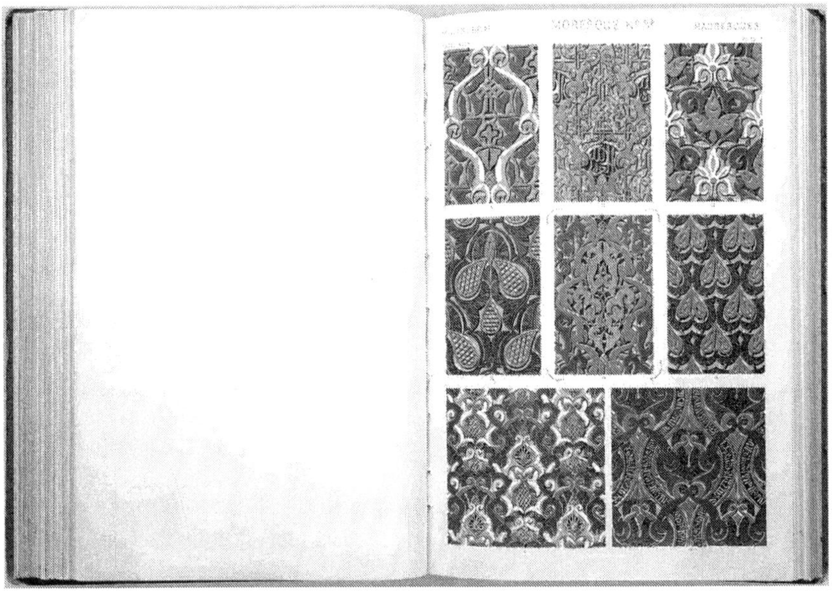

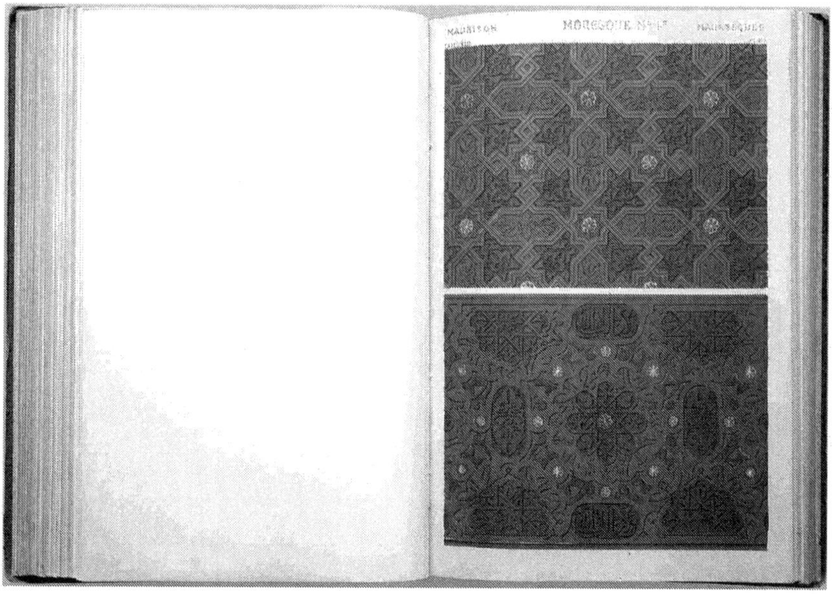
MORESQUE

Octavo

Octavo

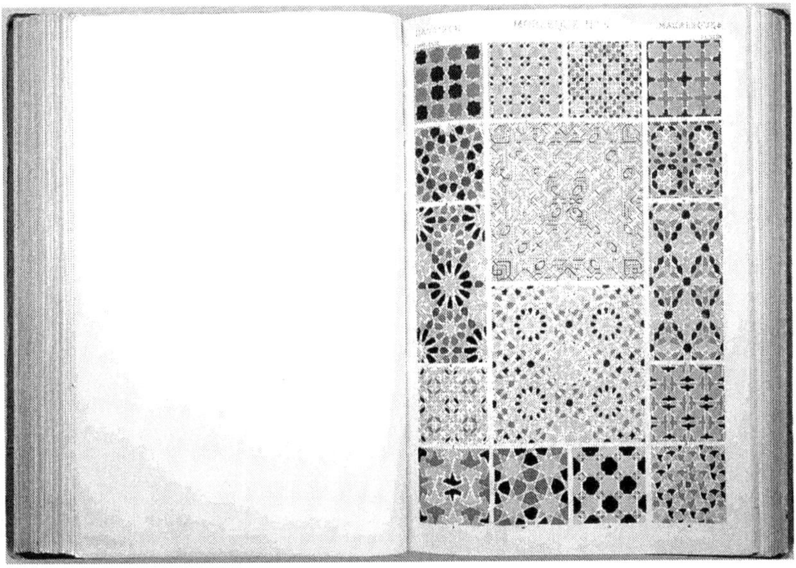

CHAPTER XI.—PLATES 44, 45, 46, 47, 47*, 48.

PERSIAN ORNAMENT.

PLATES XLIV., XLV., XLVI.

[illegible]

PLATES XLVII., XLVII*.

[illegible]

PLATE XLVIII.

[illegible]

[illegible]

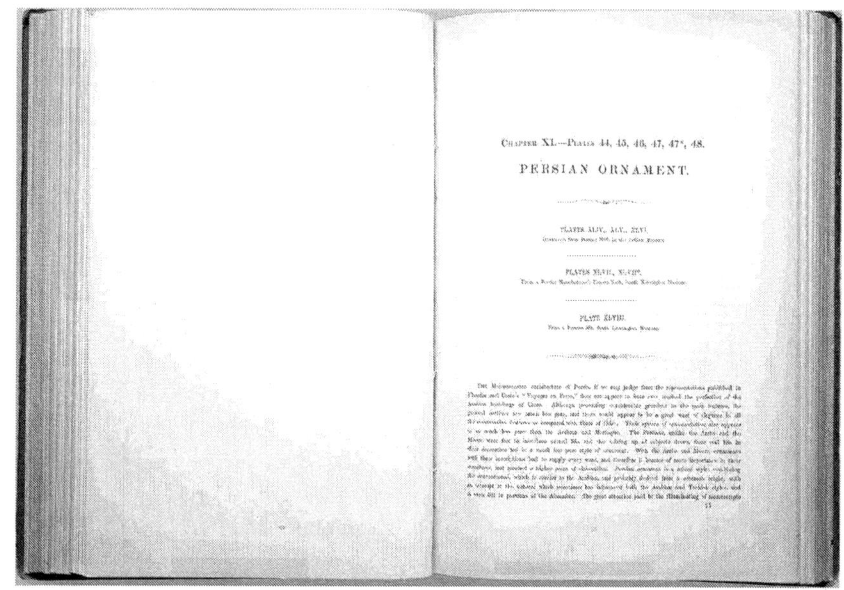

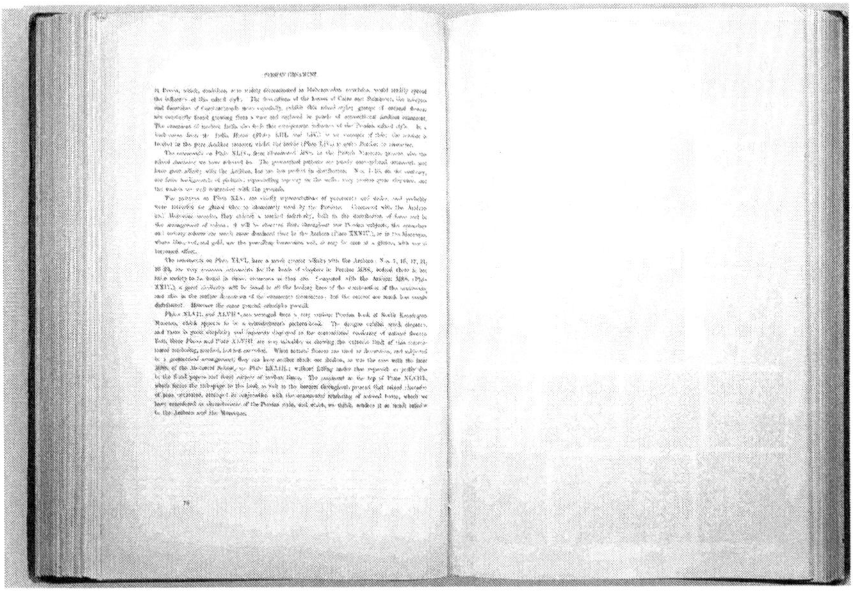

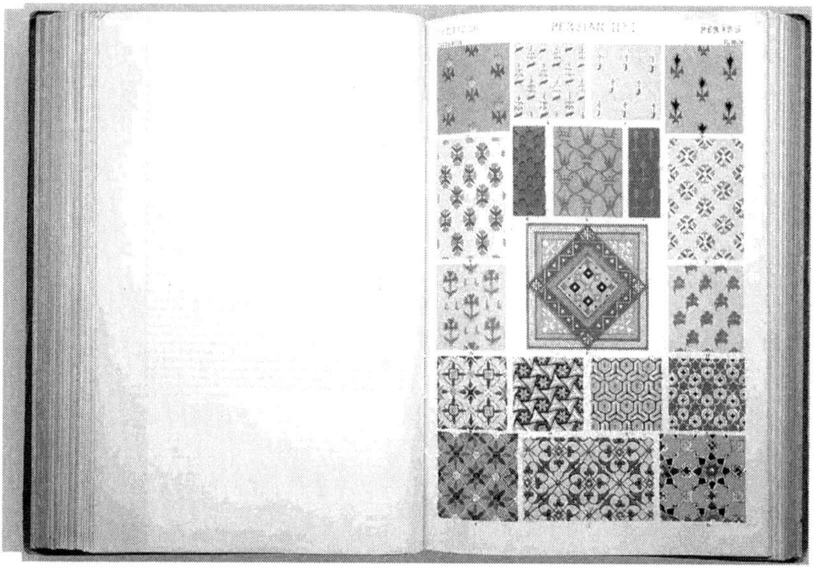

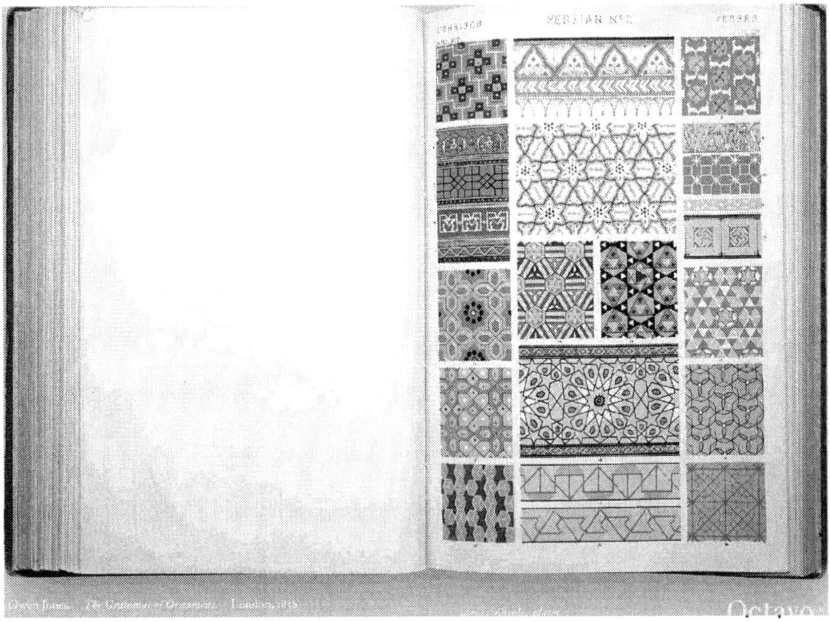
PERSIAN
Owen Jones
The Grammar of Ornament
London
Octavo

PERSIAN Nº 3

PERSIAN Nº 4.

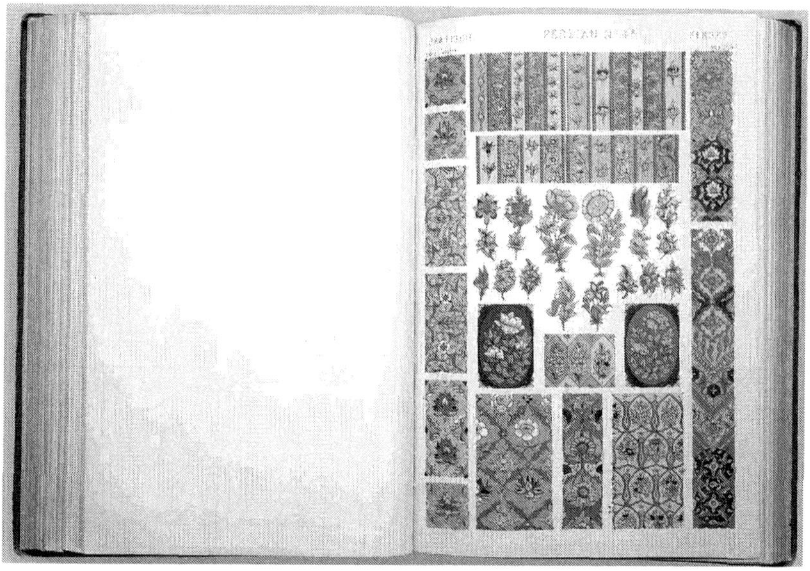

PERSIAN Nº 8.
Owen Jones. The Grammar of Ornament. London, 1856.
Octavo

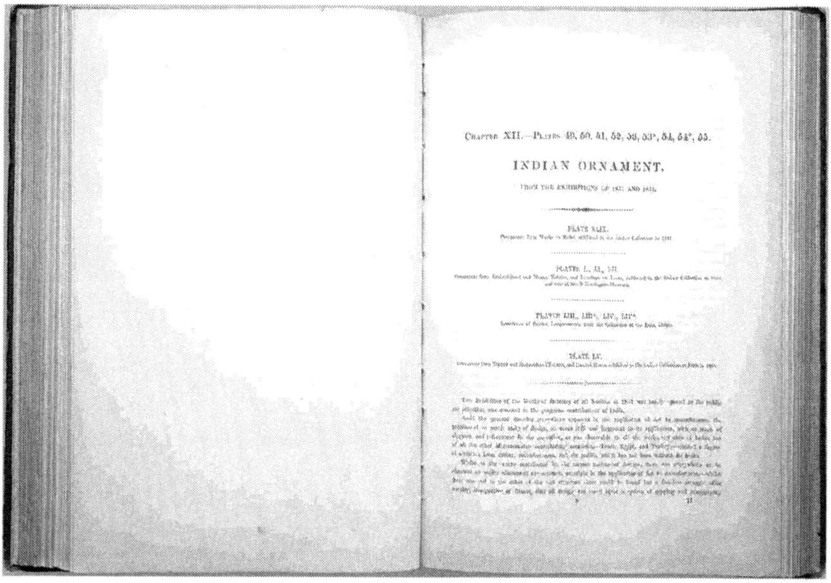
CHAPTER XII.—PLATES 49, 50, 51, 52, 53, 53*, 54, 54*, 55.
INDIAN ORNAMENT.
PLATE XLIX.
PLATE LV.

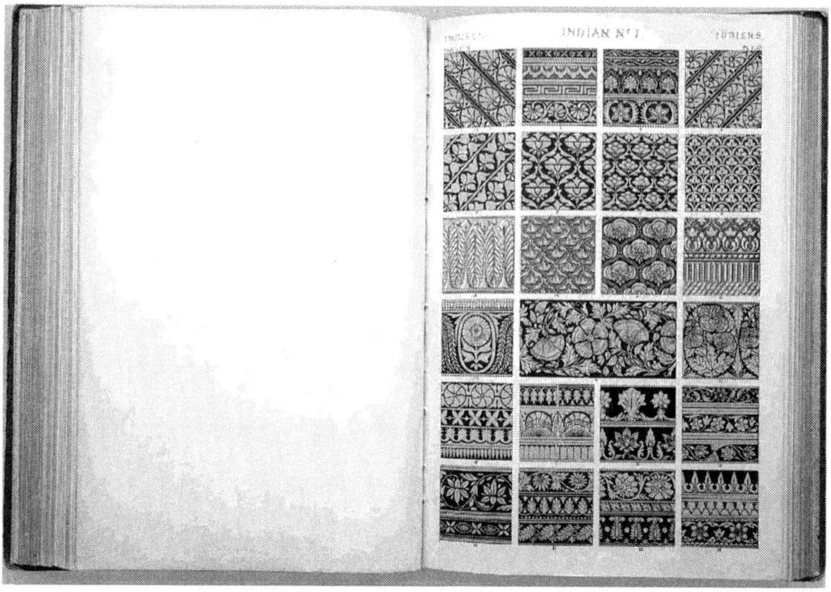
INDIAN Nº 1.

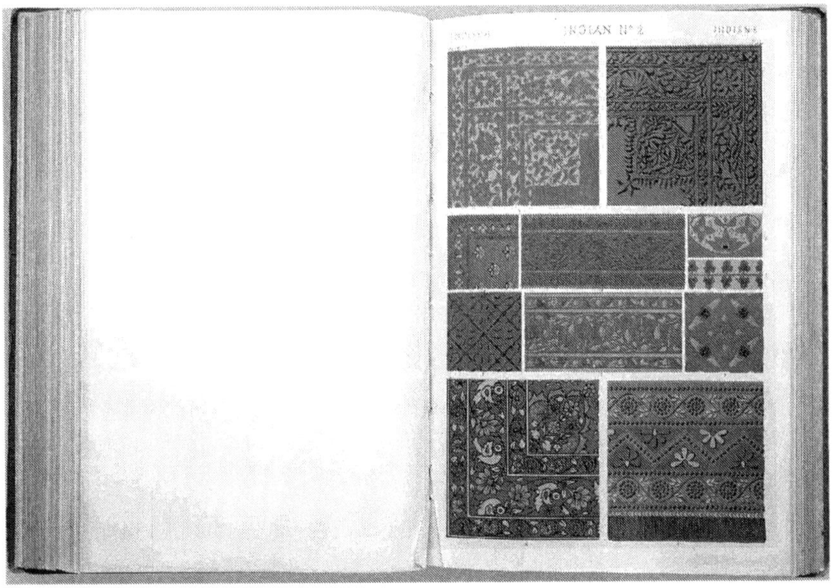
INDIAN Nº 2
INDIENS

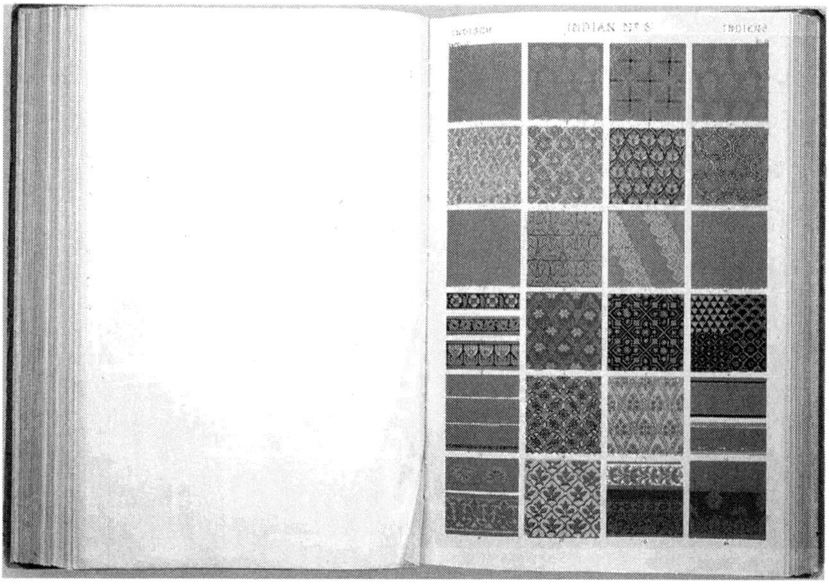
INDIAN No 8

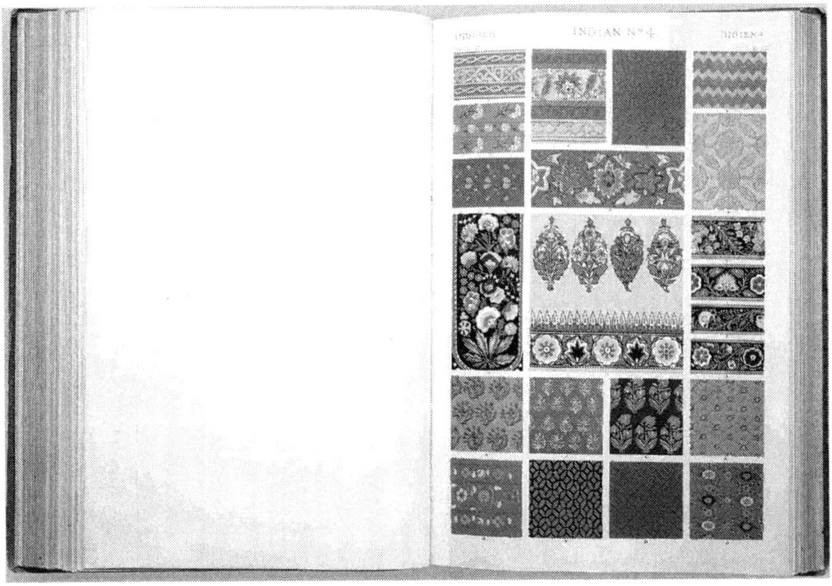
INDIAN Nº 4.

INDIAN

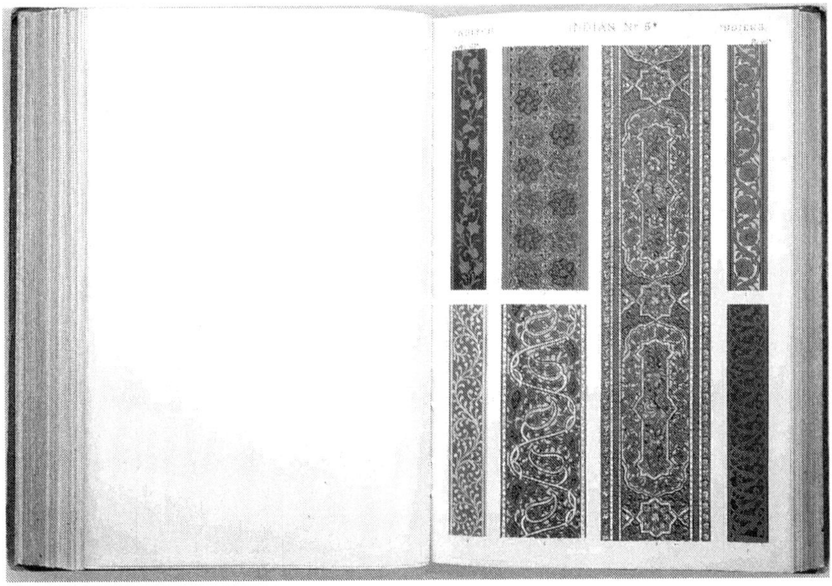
INDIAN Nº 5*

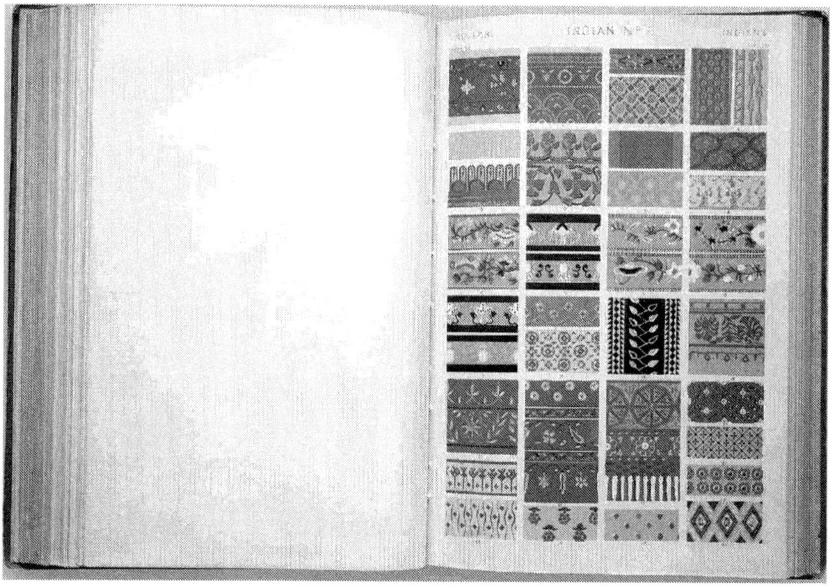

Chapter XIII.—Plates 56, 57, 58.

HINDOO ORNAMENT.

Plate LVI.

[illegible]

Plate LVII.

[illegible]

Plate LVIII.

[illegible]

[illegible]

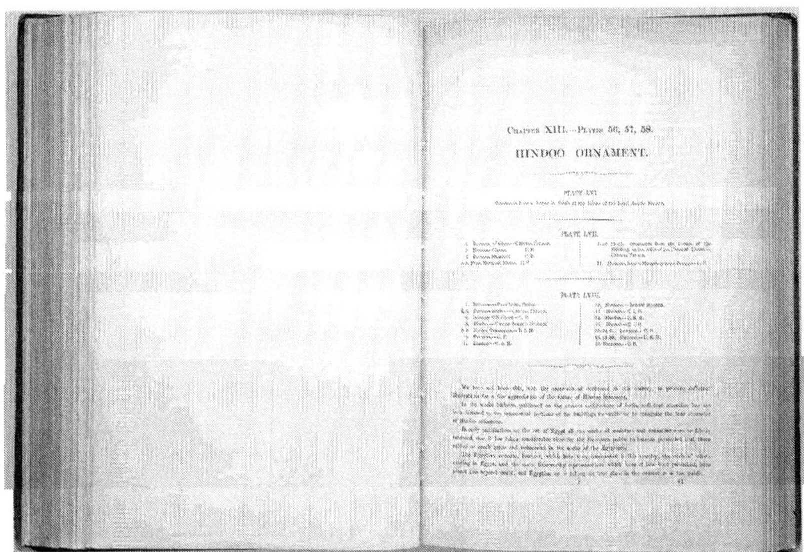

When the [illegible] shall have been done for the ancient architecture of India, we shall be in a better position than we are at present [illegible] for it is [illegible] or whether the Hindus are [illegible] grotesque and barbaric sculpture.

Had we possessed only [illegible] of the Parthenon, and the Temples of [illegible], we should [illegible] that the Romans were far greater architects than the Greeks. But the [illegible] of a single moulding from the Parthenon would at once [illegible] the judgment, and [illegible] that we were studying the works of a people who had reached the highest point in civilisation and refinement.

Although ornament is [illegible] to architecture, and should never be allowed to [illegible] or be [illegible] it is to ornament [illegible] of an architectural monument; and by the [illegible] the [illegible] of the [illegible]. All [illegible] of the [illegible] of a building [illegible].

No one can peruse the Essay on Hindu Architecture by Ram Raz* without feeling that a higher state of architectural perfection [illegible] than the works published up to the present time would lead us to believe. In this work not only are [illegible] but also minute directions are given for the [illegible] and [illegible] well preserved.

One of the precepts quoted by Ram Raz [illegible] the general [illegible] of [illegible] in building an edifice, therefore, let all its parts, from the basement to the roof, be duly considered."

Among the directions for the [illegible] proportions of columns, bases and capitals is a rule for fixing the proper diminution of the upper diameter of the column in proportion to the base.

Ram Raz says, that the general rule adopted by the Hindu architects was to divide the diameter of the column at the base by as many parts as there were diameters in the whole height of the column, and that one of these parts was invariably deducted [illegible] from the upper diameter. From which it is apparent that the higher the column the [illegible] the [illegible] of the [illegible] of columns of the same proportion [illegible] according to the height.

The best specimens of Hindu ornament we have been able to procure are represented in Plate LXI., from a [illegible] of the Asiatic Society, and supposed to belong to a period between the fifth and ninth century A.D. The ornaments are very beautifully executed, and [illegible] Greek influence. The ornament No. 8 represents the lotus, seen as it were in plan, with the bud in [illegible] at the back of the [illegible].

In the sacred books quoted by Ram Raz are several directions to ornament the various mouldings [illegible] which seem to be the chief types of the decorations on the mouldings.

The architectural features of Hindu buildings consist chiefly of mouldings [illegible] in the varying proportions of [illegible] it is evident that the whole value of the style will consist in the [illegible] with which these mouldings are effected; but, as we said before, we have no opportunity of judging how far this is the case.

* "Essay on the Architecture of the Hindus." By Ram Raz. London, [illegible].

On Plate LXII. we have gathered together all the examples of [illegible] ornament that we could find in the copies of the paintings from the Caves of [illegible], exhibited by the East India Company at the Crystal Palace. As these copies, notwithstanding that they are said to be faithful, are yet by a European hand, it is difficult to say how far they may be relied upon. In the other Hindu pictures, such as [illegible], at all events, there is so little [illegible] character that they might belong to any style. It is [illegible] that in these paintings there should be so little ornament; a peculiarity that we have [illegible] paintings in the possession of the Asiatic Society. There is a remarkable absence of ornament even on the dresses of the figures.

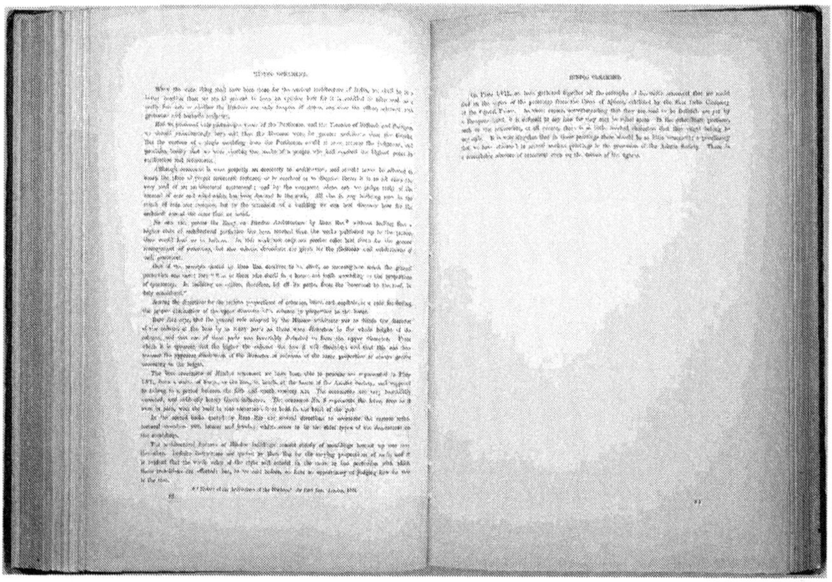

HINDOO Nº1

HINDOO Nº3

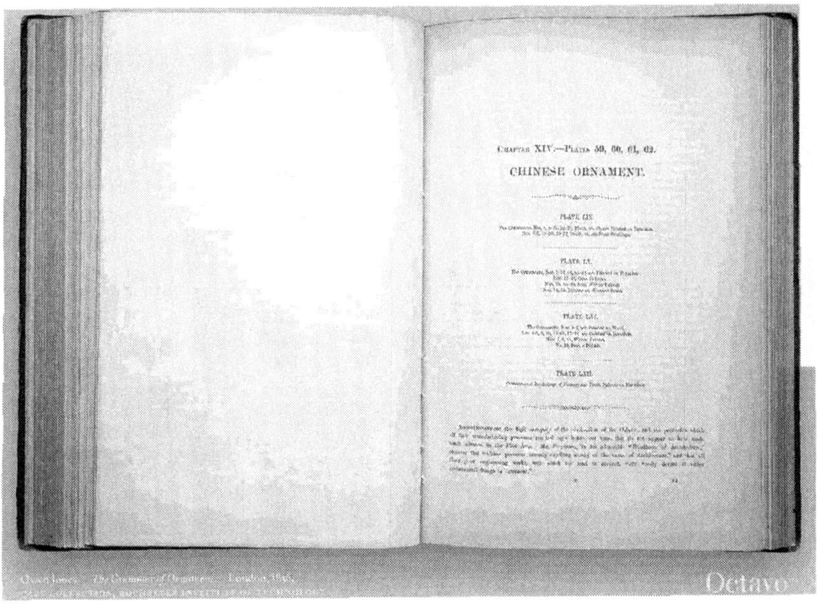
Chapter XIV.—Plates 59, 60, 61, 62.
CHINESE ORNAMENT.
Octavo

[illegible] through the [illegible] articles of every kind which have been imported into this country, they do not appear to have gone beyond that [illegible] stage of civilisation. [illegible] the *New Zealanders*; [illegible] with all [illegible] nations, the happy instinct [illegible] [illegible] each other's efforts.

The general forms of many of the Chinese porcelain vases are remarkable for the beauty of their outline, [illegible] the Nile, [illegible] the pure form of the Chinese vase is often destroyed by the addition of [illegible] or other excrescent ornaments [illegible], but to a minor degree.

In their decoration, both painted and woven, the Chinese exhibit [illegible]. The designs on Plate LXIX., [illegible] Nos. 1, 8, 13, 18, 19, [illegible] Nos. 28, 31, [illegible] and the other patterns of this class on the Plates [illegible] the Chinese share with the Indian this happy power in their woven fabrics; [illegible] The Chinese are [illegible] colour and the most delicate shades.

They are not only successful in the use of the primaries, but also of the secondaries and tertiaries, most successful, perhaps, of all in the management of the lightest tones of pure colour, [illegible] pale green, [illegible].

Of purely ornamental or conventional forms, other than geometric patterns, the Chinese possess but very few. On Plate LX. are some examples in Nos. 3, 7, 8. They have no floating conventional ornament [illegible] supplied by a representation of natural flowers [illegible] Nos. 11, 19, Plate LXI.; [illegible] see Plate LXII. In all cases, however, [illegible] In their painted [illegible] we are not shocked by an [illegible]. In their floral patterns, however, they always observe the [illegible] it is the least [illegible] upon this class observation which is [illegible].

We have already referred in the Greek chapter to the peculiarities of the Chinese fretwork. [illegible]

[illegible] Plate LXI. [illegible] Nos. 3, 8, 18, [illegible]; No. 1, Plate LX., [illegible].

On the whole, Chinese ornament is a very faithful expression of the nature of this peculiar people; its characteristic feature is [illegible] the Chinese are totally [illegible], and all their works are accordingly [illegible] in the highest grace of art, — the ideal.

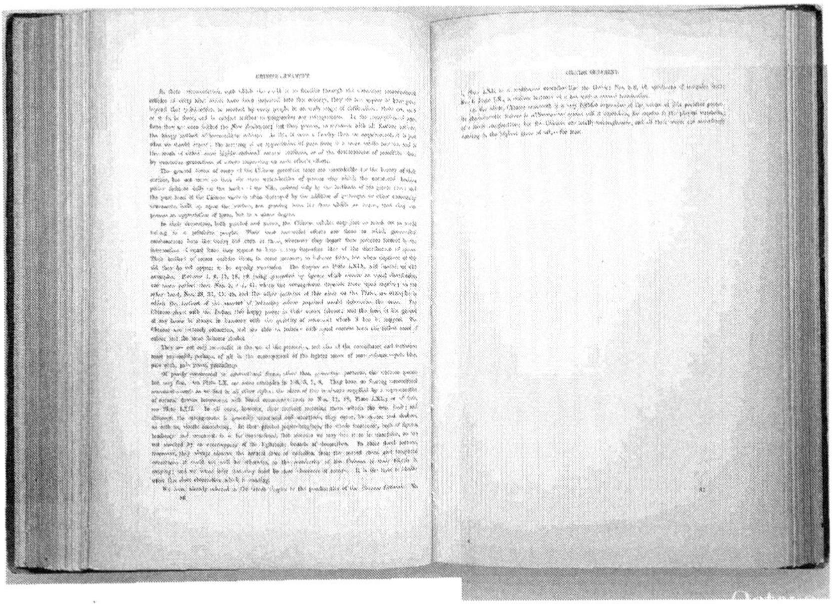

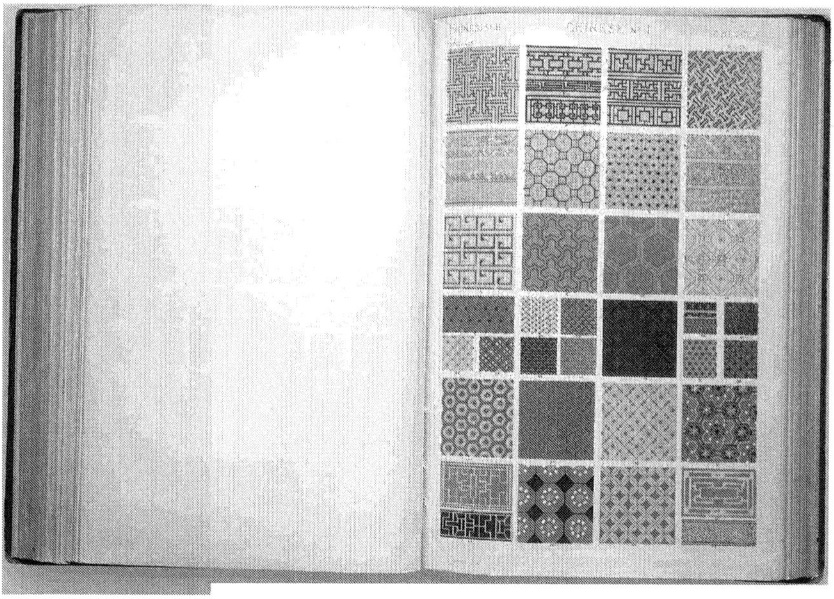

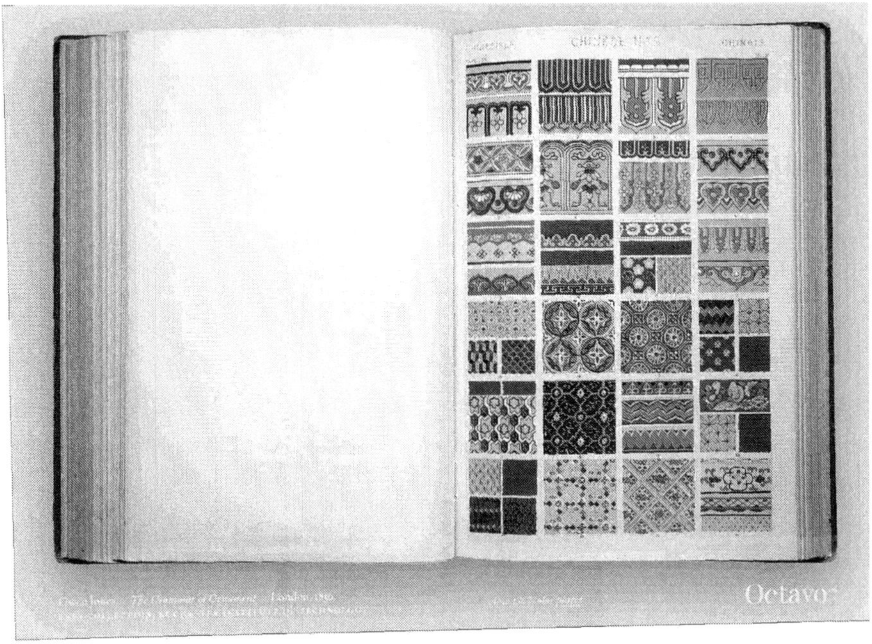
Octavo

CHINESE Nº 4
Octavo

CHAPTER XV.—PLATES 63, 64, 65.
CELTIC ORNAMENT.
PLATE LXIII.
LAPIDARY ORNAMENTATION.
PLATE LXIV.
INTERLACED STYLE.
Octavo

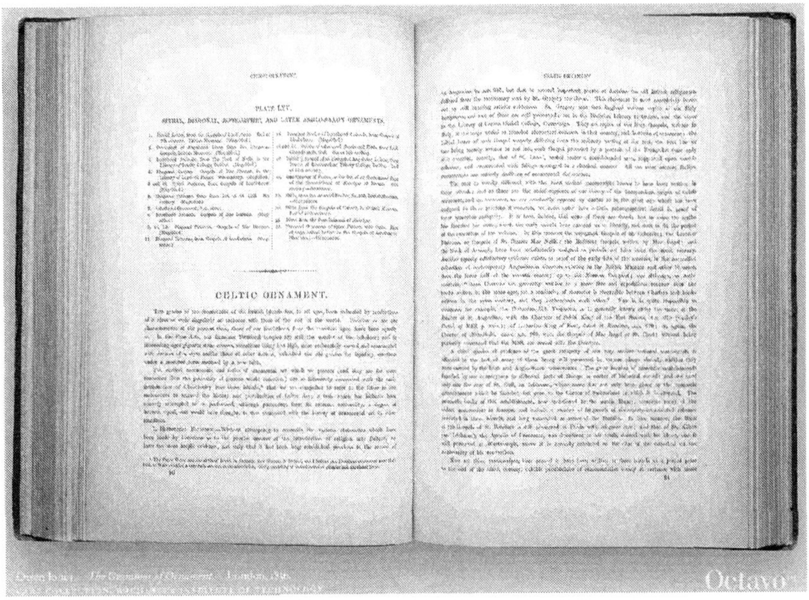
PLATE LXV.
CELTIC ORNAMENT.
Octavo

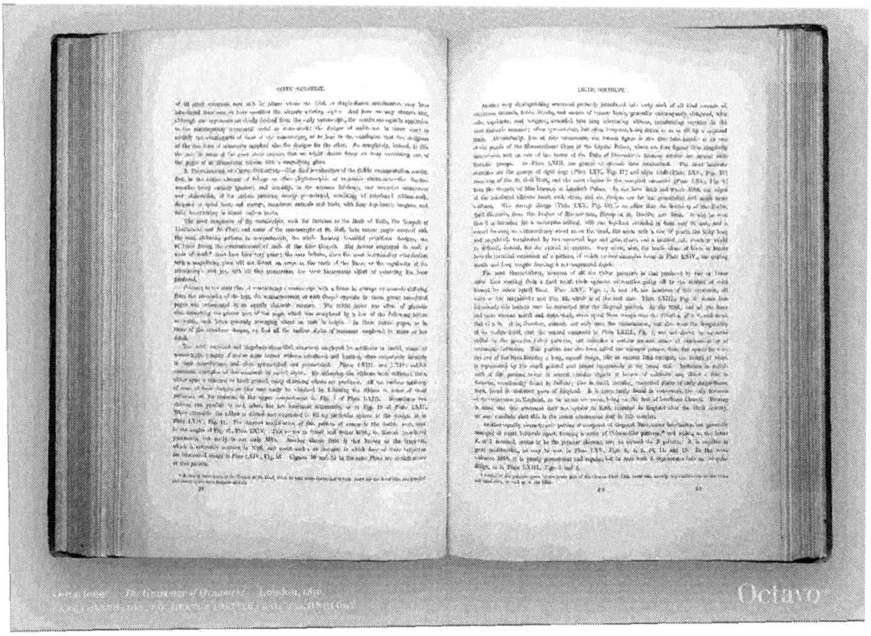
Octavo

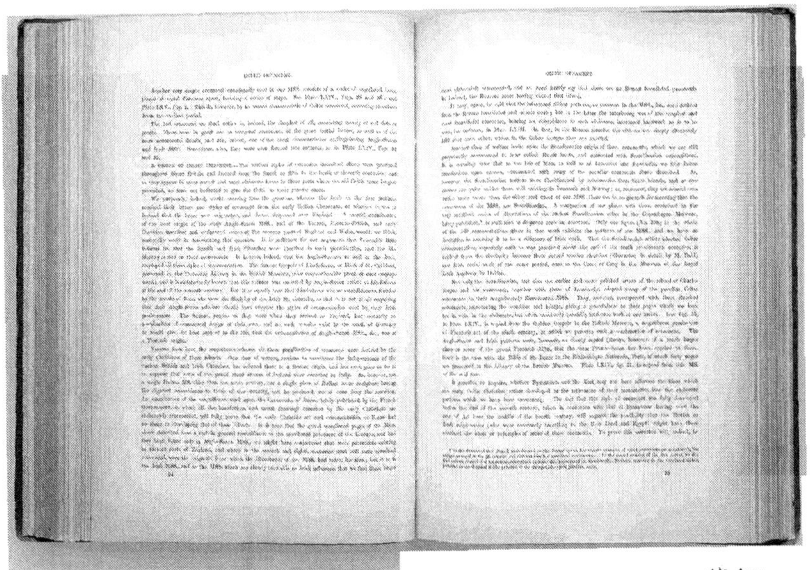

Owen Jones, The Grammar of Ornament, London 1856

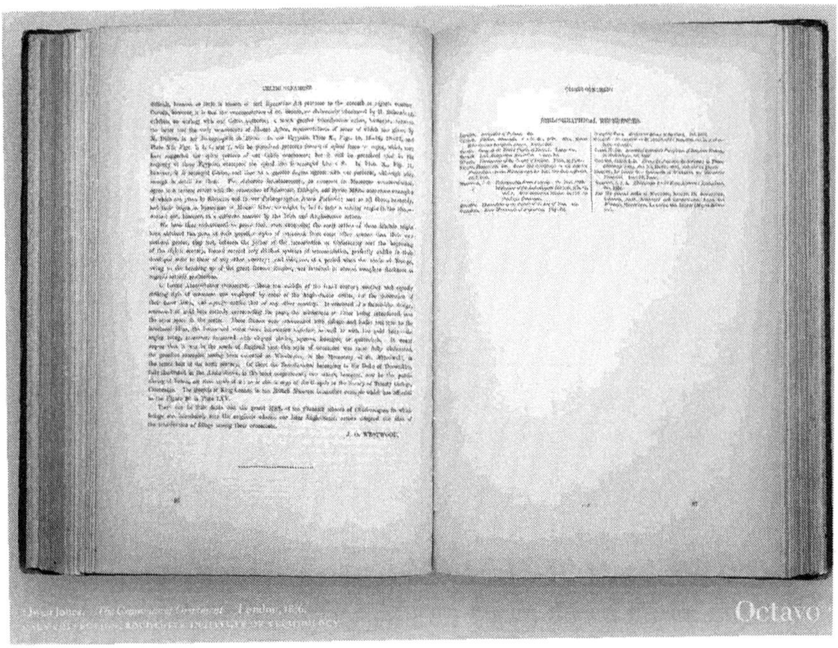
Octavo

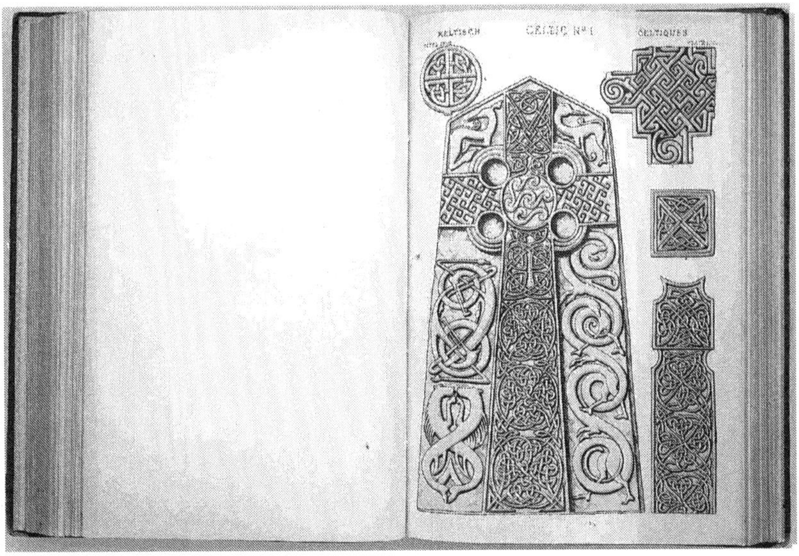
KELTISCH
CELTIC Nº 1
CELTIQUES

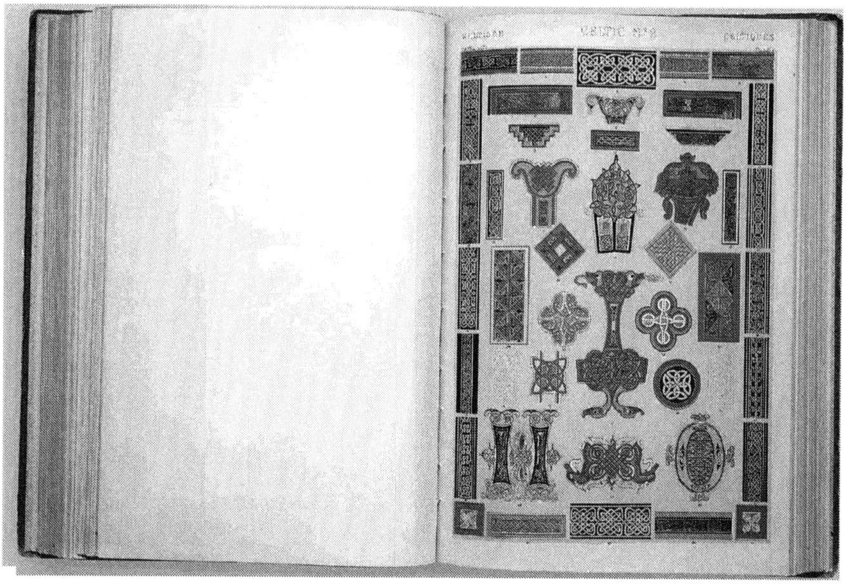

CELTIC No 3
Octavo

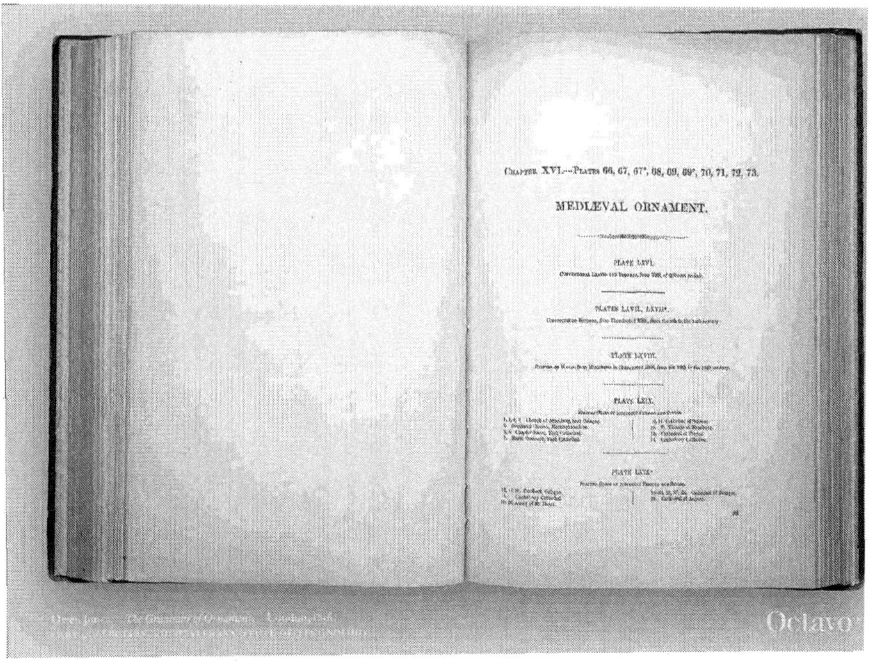
CHAPTER XVI.—PLATES 66, 67, 67*, 68, 69, 69*, 70, 71, 72, 73.
MEDIÆVAL ORNAMENT.
PLATE LXVI.
PLATES LXVII, LXVII*.
PLATE LXVIII.
PLATE LXIX.
PLATE LXIX*.
Octavo

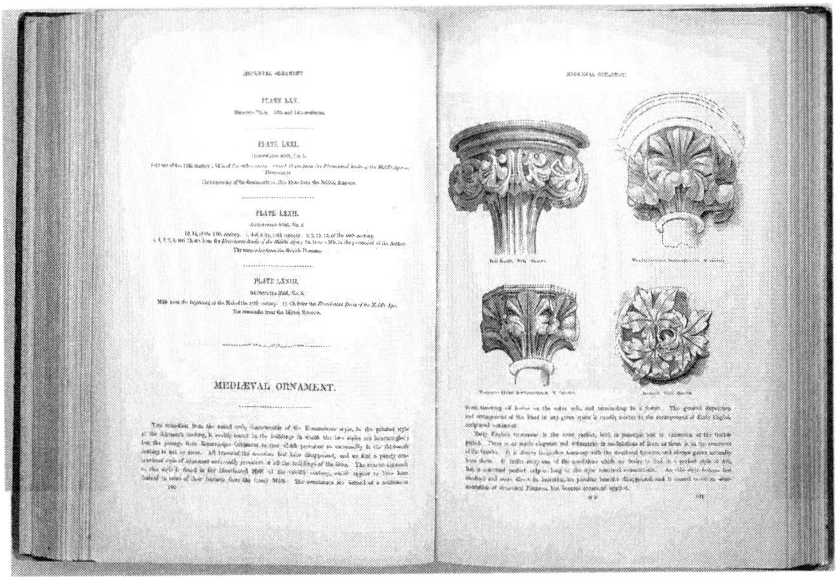
PLATE LXX.

PLATE LXXI.

PLATE LXXII.

PLATE LXXIII.

MEDIÆVAL ORNAMENT.

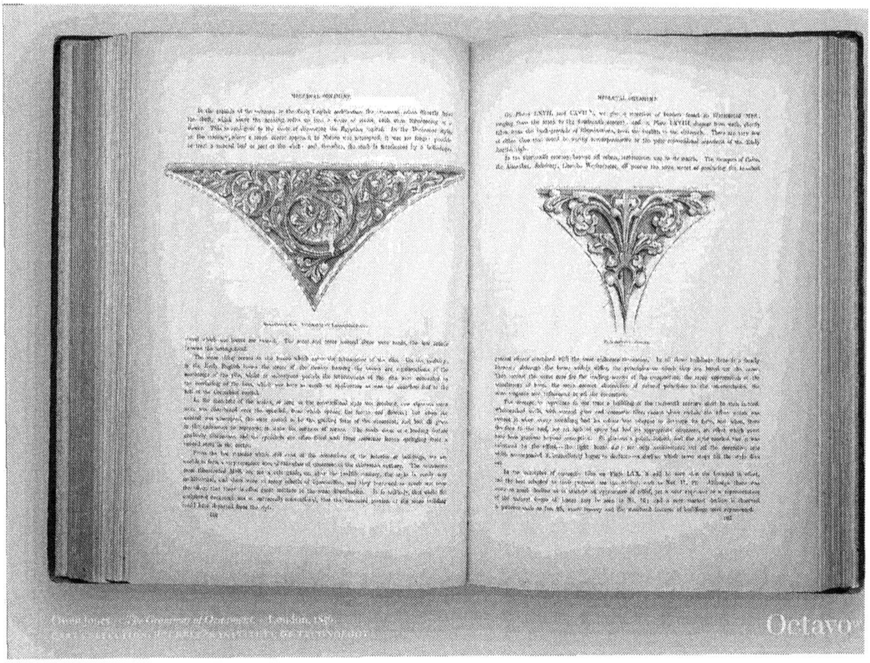
Octavo

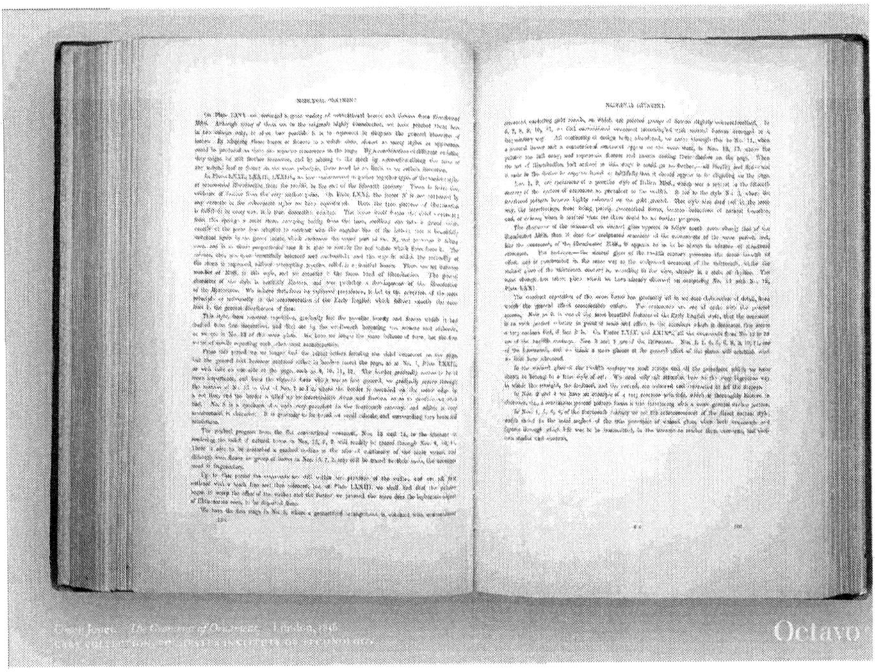
Octavo

MIDDLE AGES
Octavo

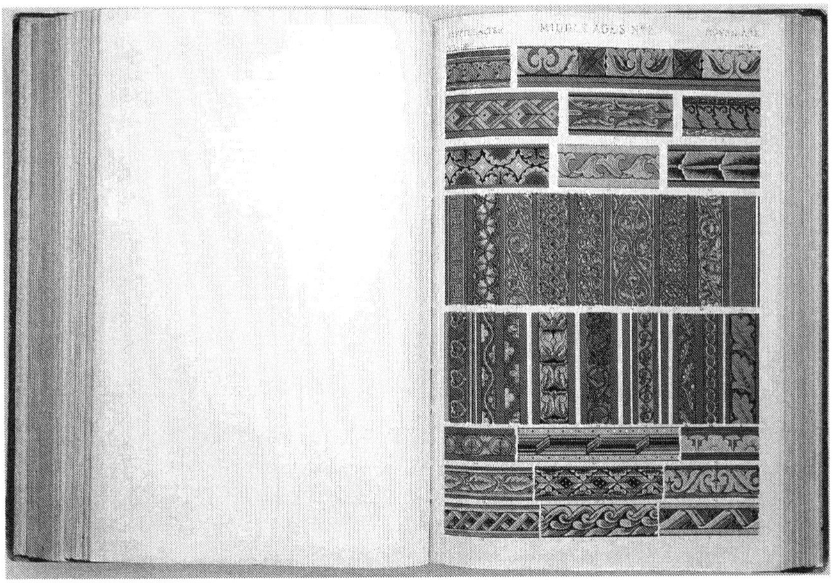

MIDDLE AGES

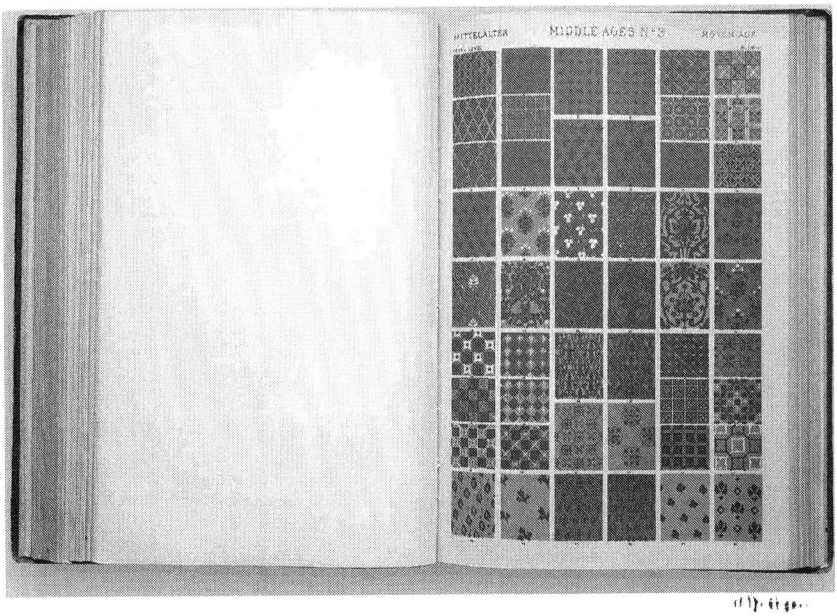
MIDDLE AGES

STAINED GLASS
Octavo

Octavo

Octavo

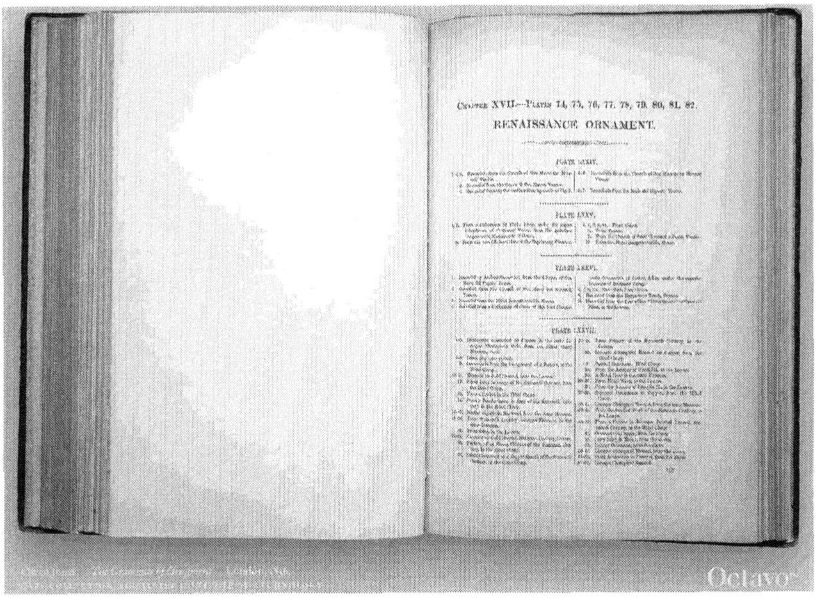
Chapter XVII.—Plates 74, 75, 76, 77, 78, 79, 80, 81, 82.
RENAISSANCE ORNAMENT.
Octavo

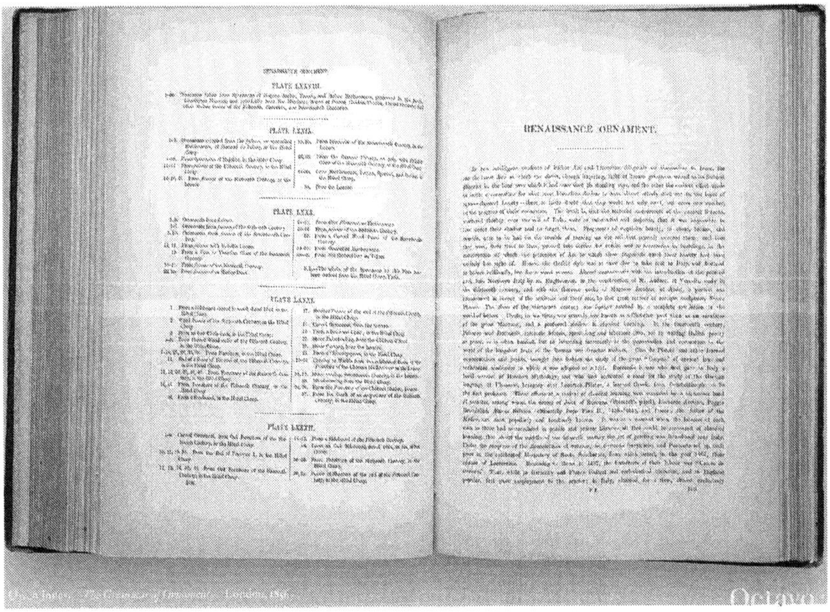
RENAISSANCE ORNAMENT.
PLATE LXXVIII.
PLATE LXXIX.
PLATE LXXX.
PLATE LXXXI.
PLATE LXXXII.
Owen Jones, The Grammar of Ornament, London, 1856
Octavo

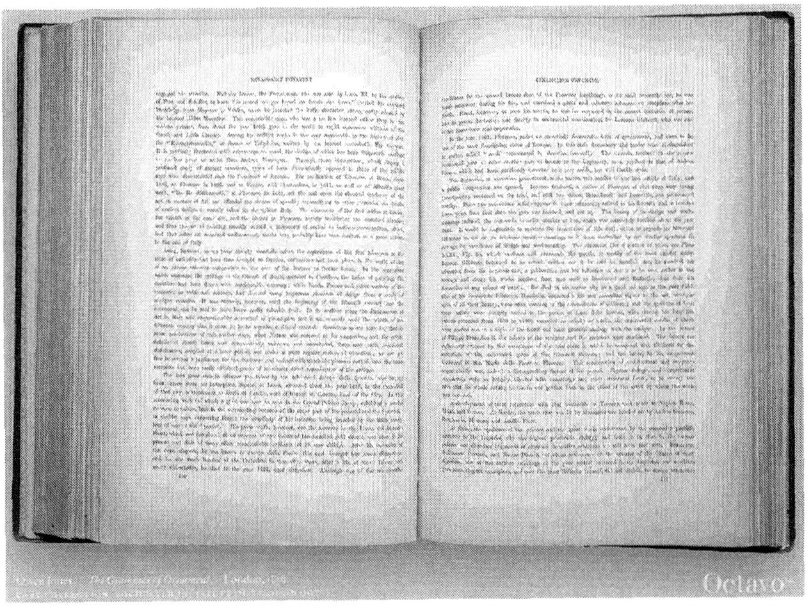
Owen Jones The Grammar of Ornament London
Octavo

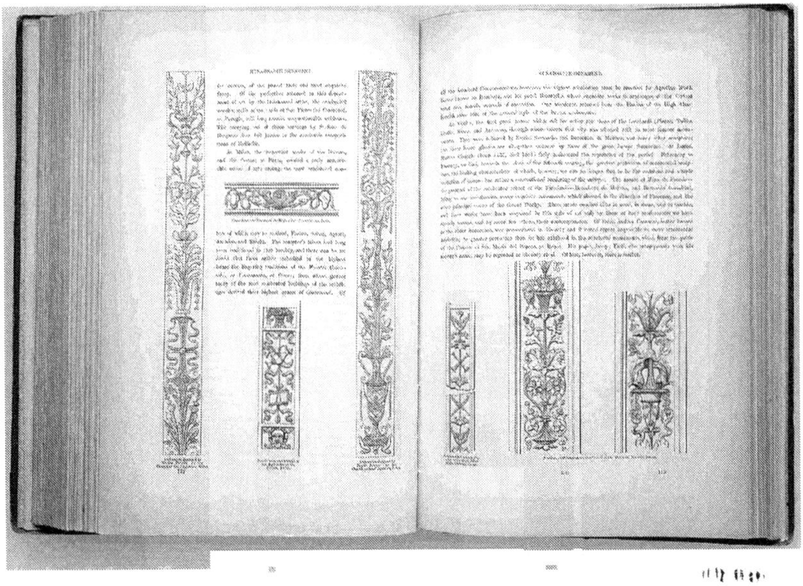

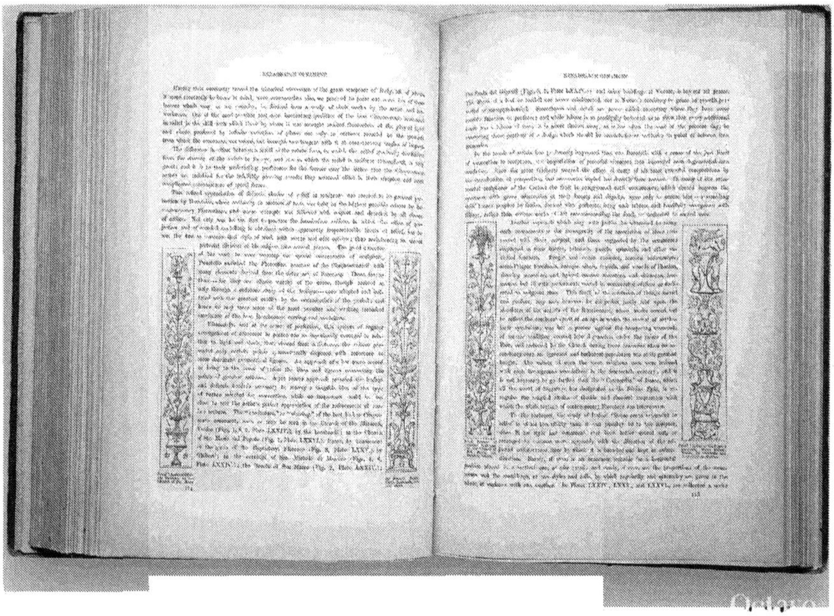

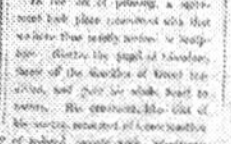

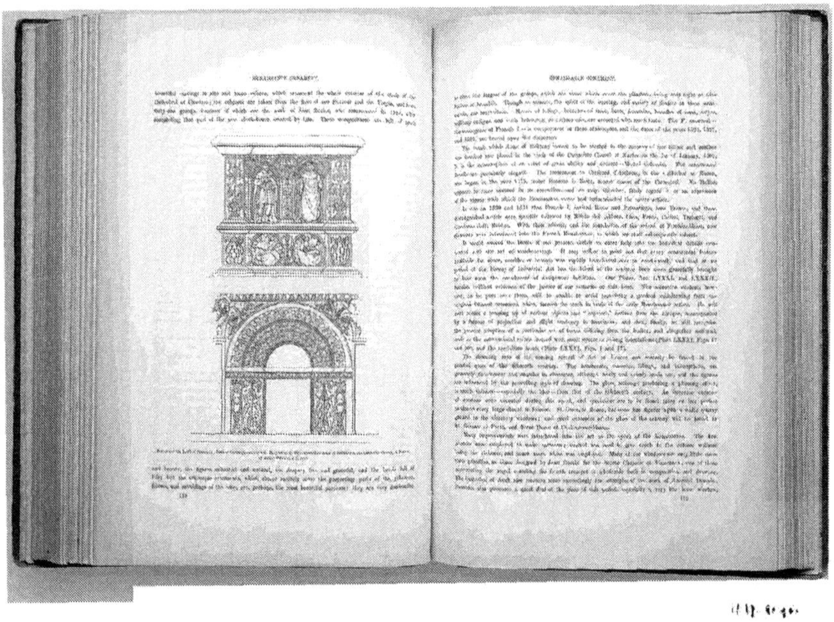

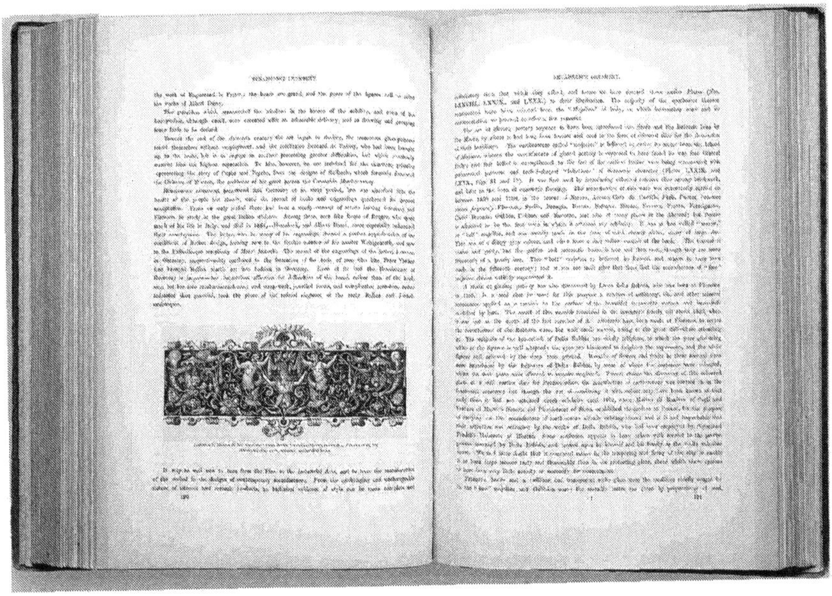

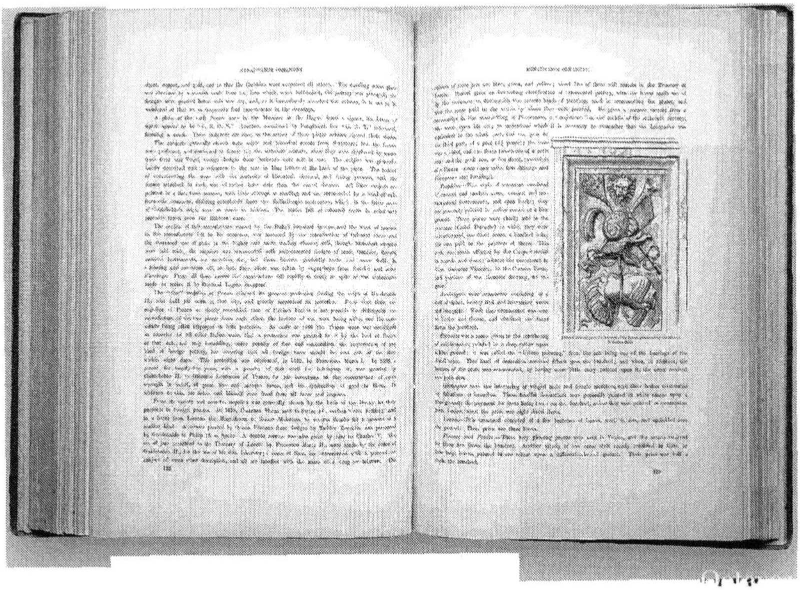

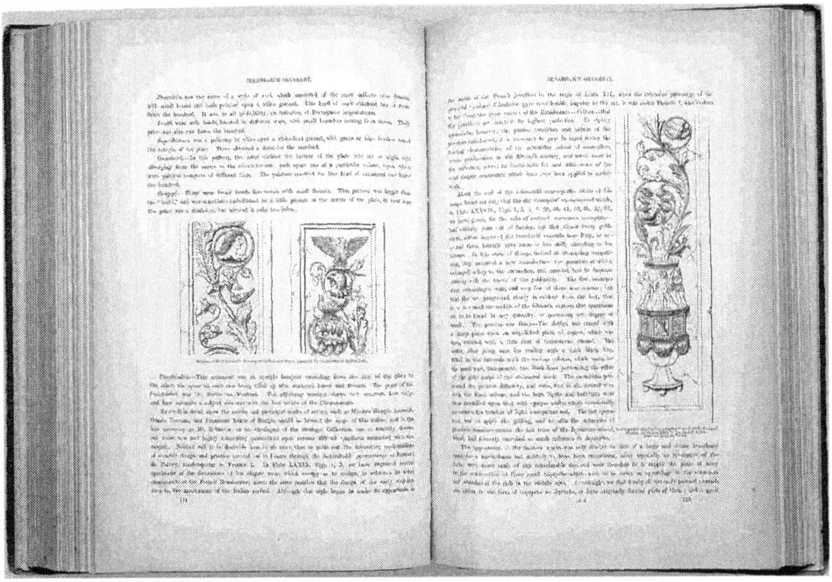

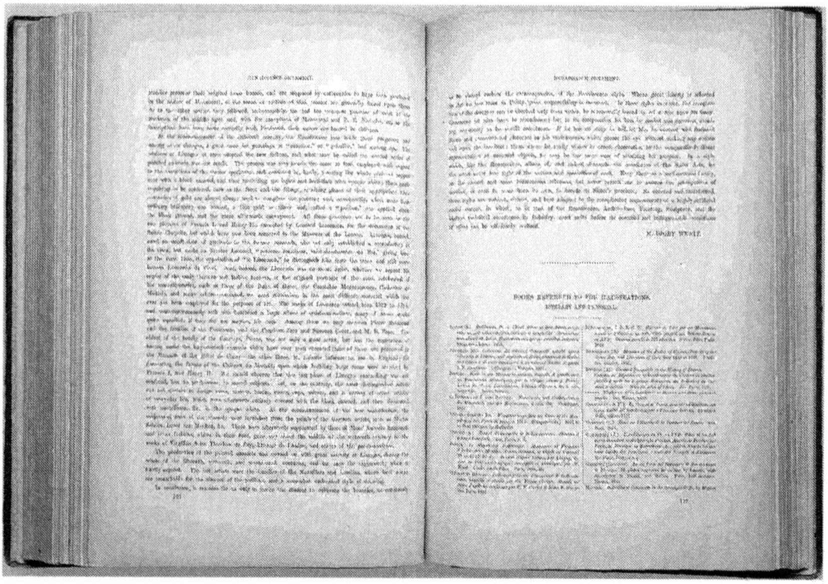

Octavo

RENAISSANCE
Octavo

RENAISSANCE Nº 2
Octavo

RENAISSANCE Nº 5
Octavo

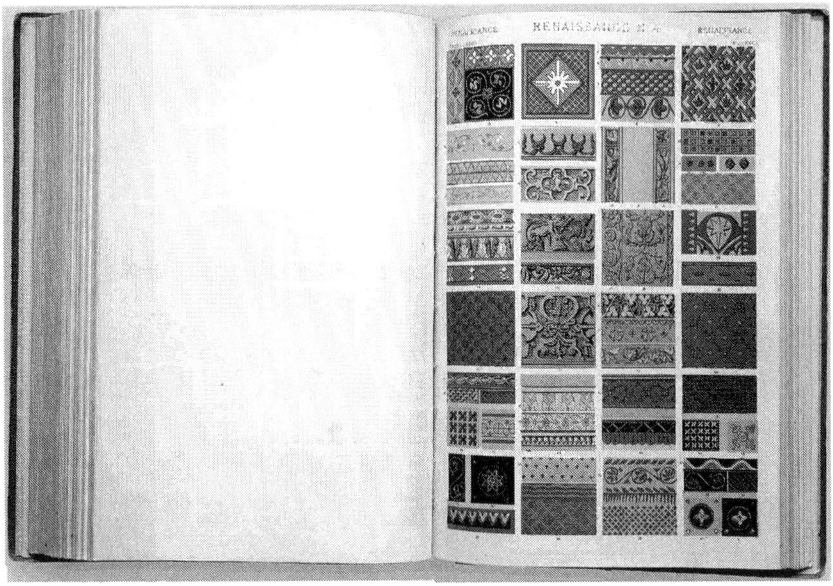
RENAISSANCE

RENAISSANCE
Octavo

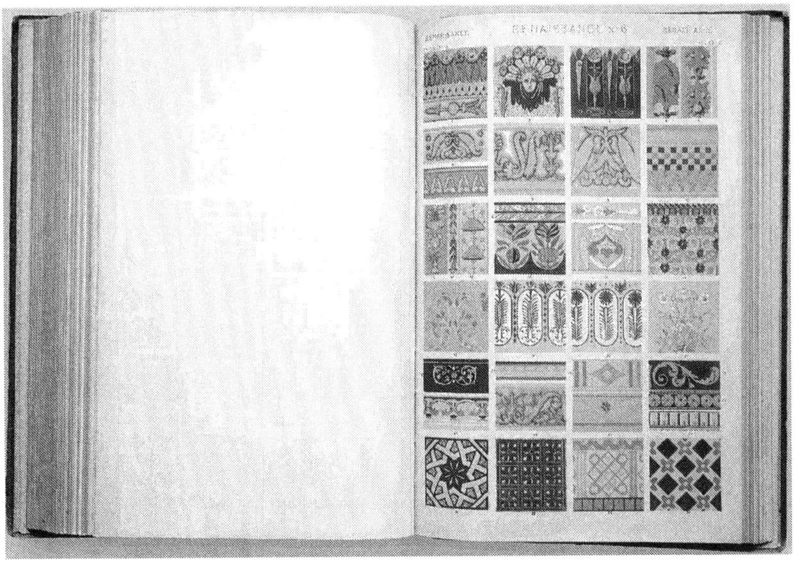

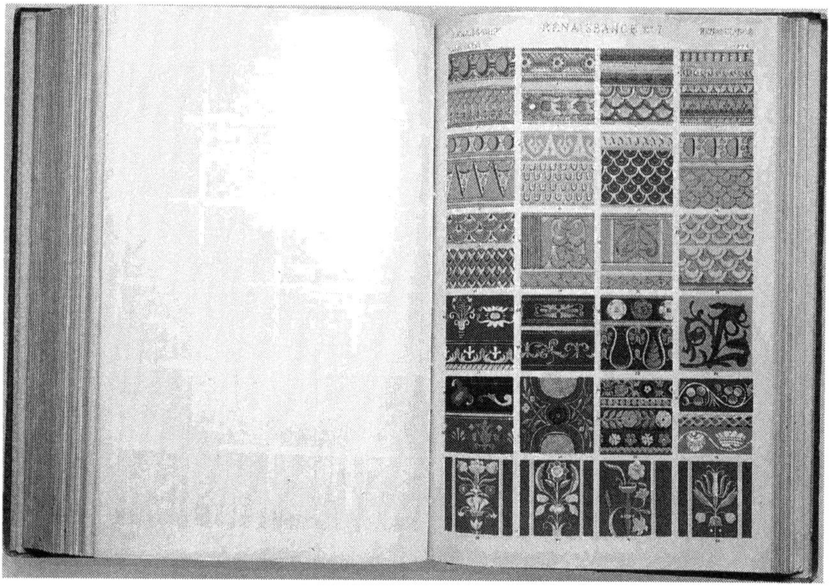
RENAISSANCE No 7

Owen Jones, The Grammar of Ornament, London

RENAISSANCE No 9
Octavo

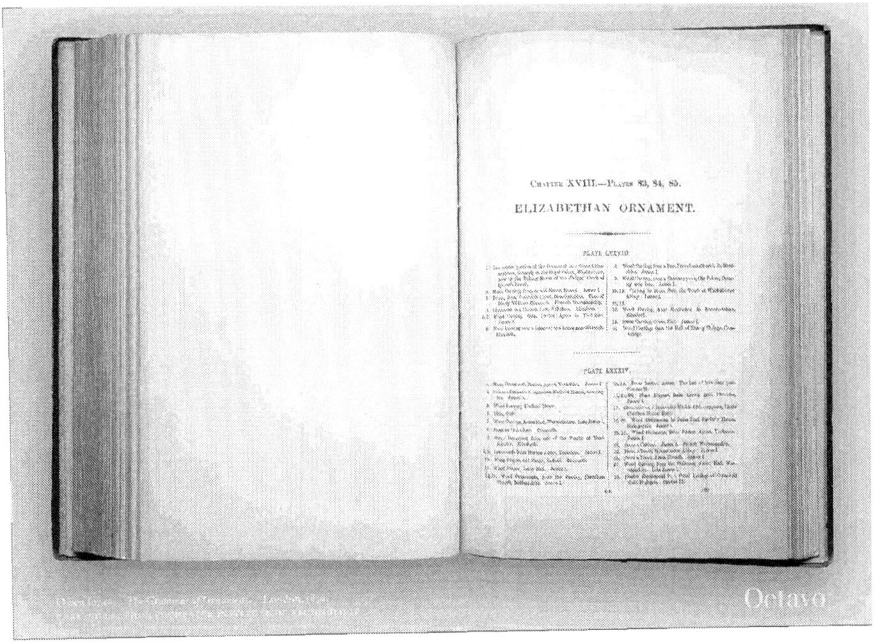
CHAPTER XVIII.—PLATES 83, 84, 85.
ELIZABETHAN ORNAMENT.
Octavo

PLATE LXXIV.

ELIZABETHAN ORNAMENT.

Octavo

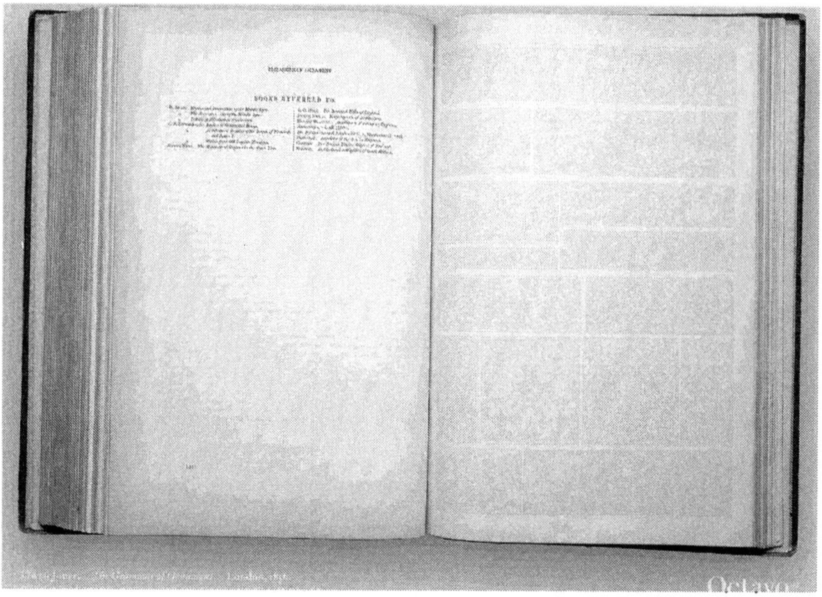
BOOKS REFERRED TO.

ELIZABETHAN Nº1

ELIZABETHAN No 2

ELIZABETHAN No 3

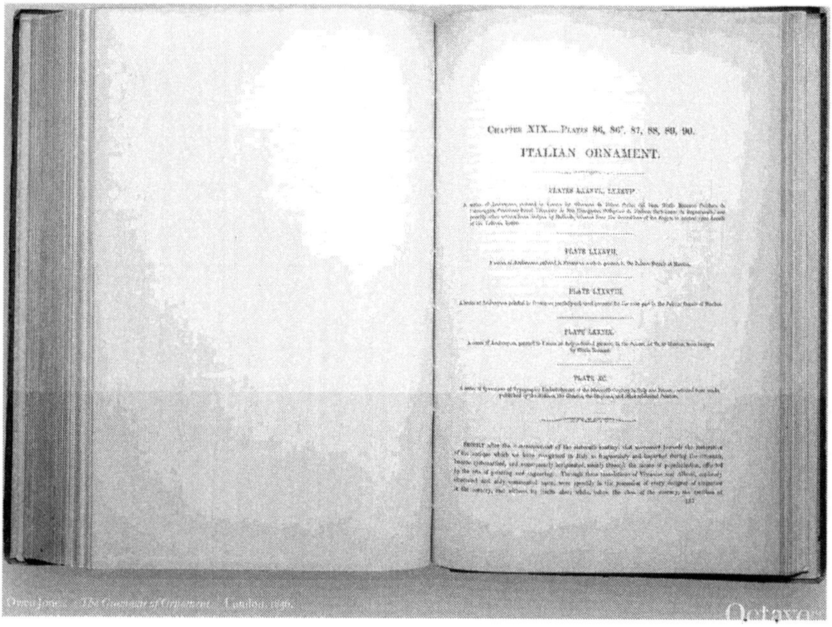
CHAPTER XIX.—PLATES 86, 86*, 87, 88, 89, 90.
ITALIAN ORNAMENT.

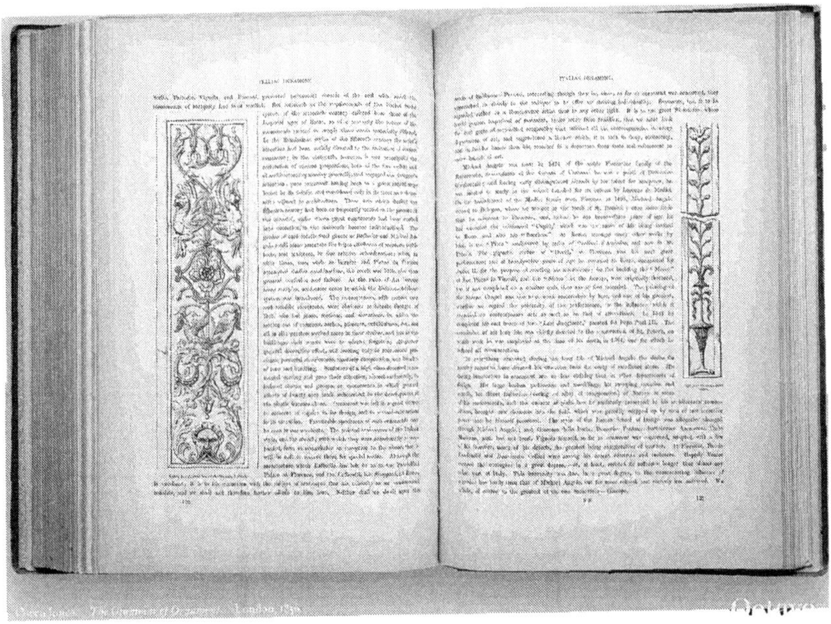

Owen Jones, The Grammar of Ornament, London 1856

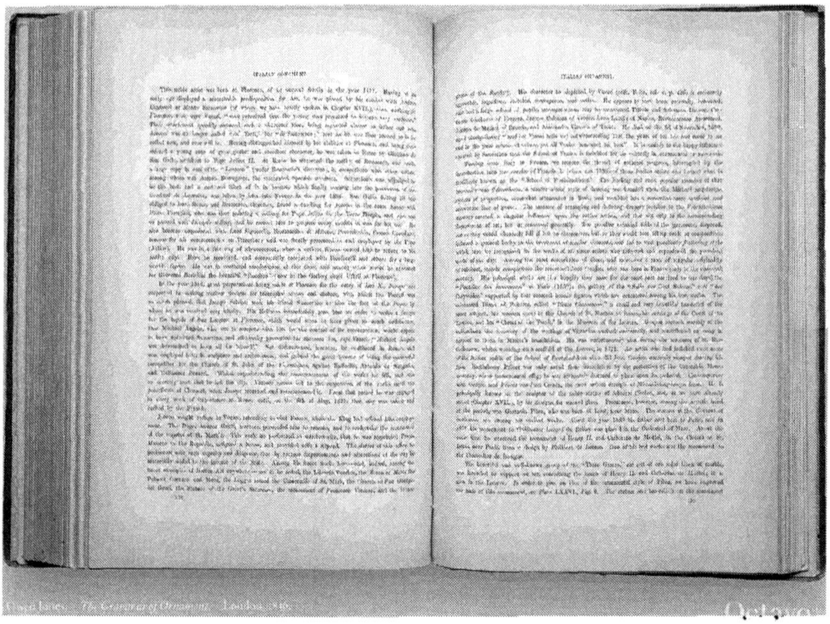
Owen Jones *The Grammar of Ornament* London

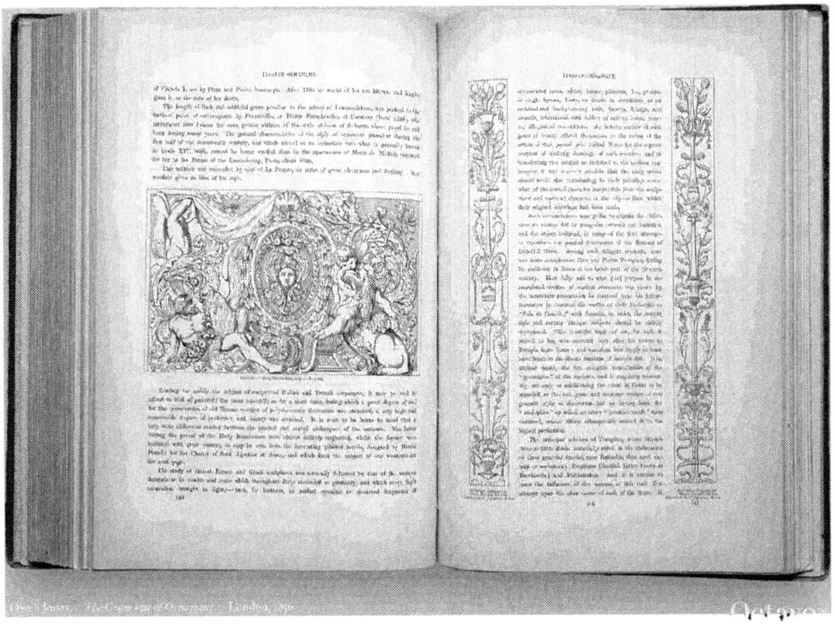

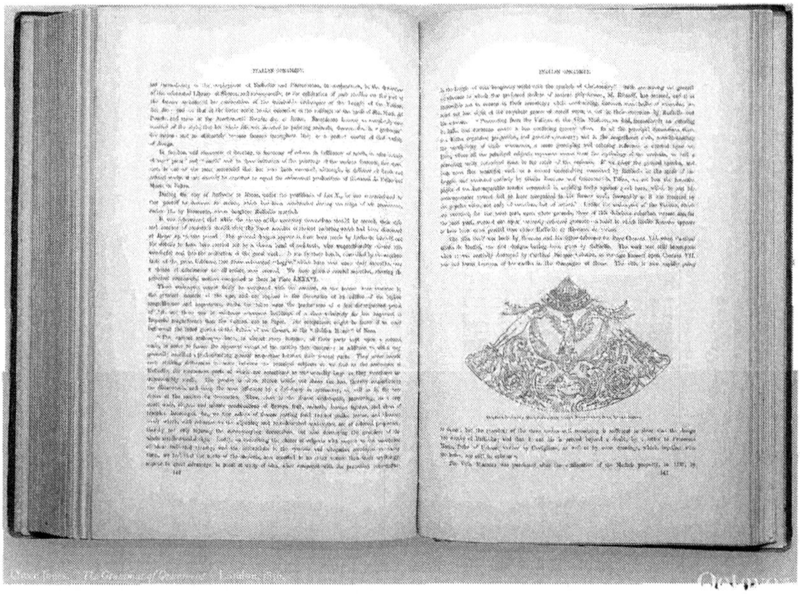

Owen Jones, *The Grammar of Ornament*, London, 1856

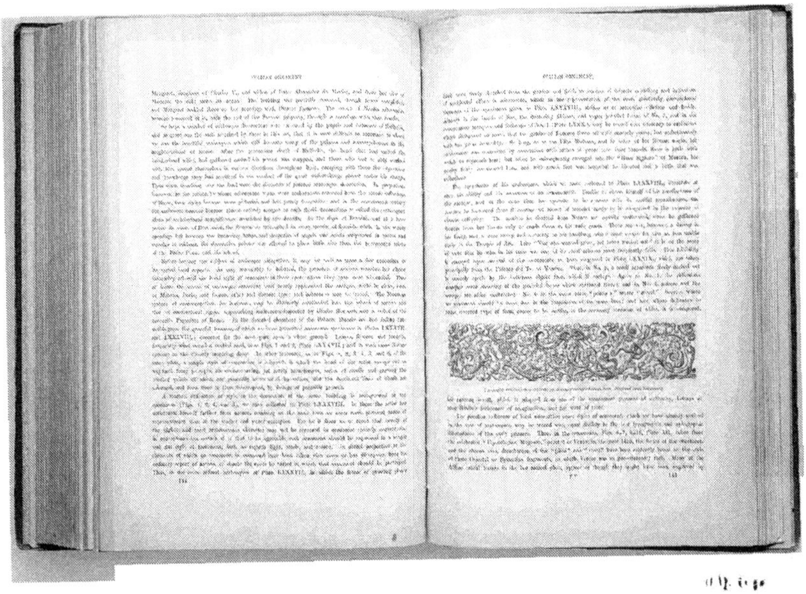

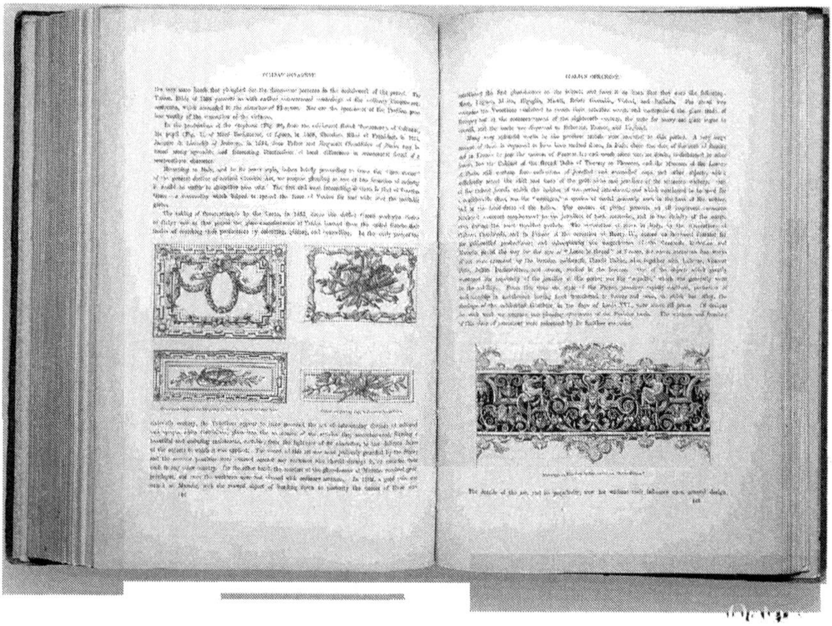

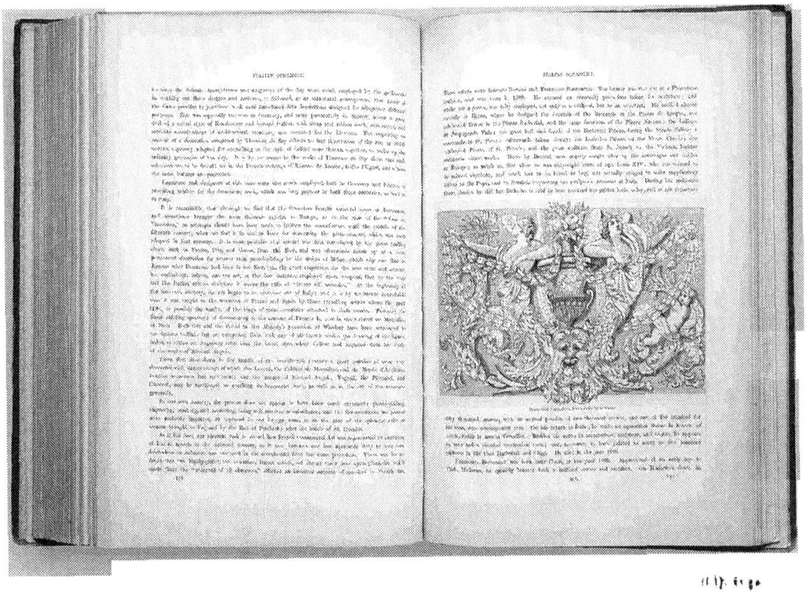

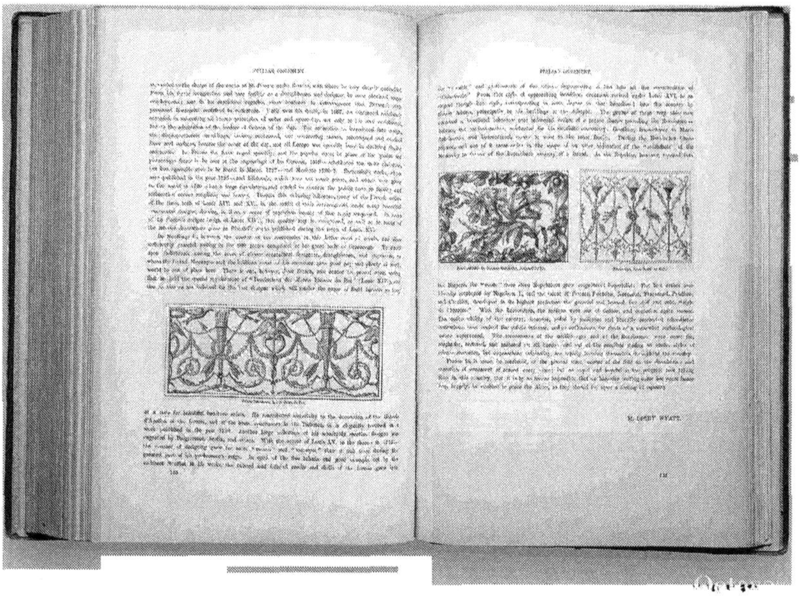
M. DIGBY WYATT

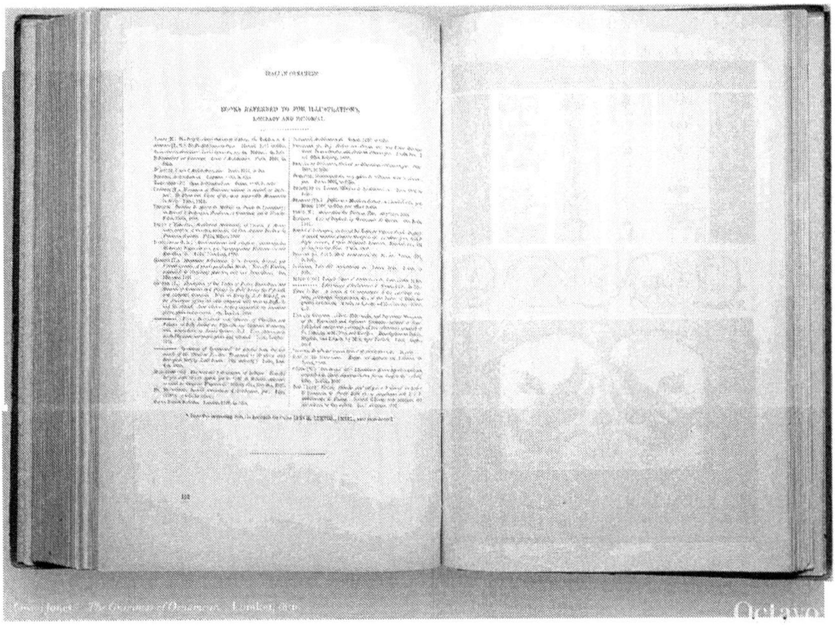
Octavo

ITALIAN Nº 1

ITALIAN N° 1

Octavo

ITALIAN

ITALIAN Nº 4

ITALIAN No 6

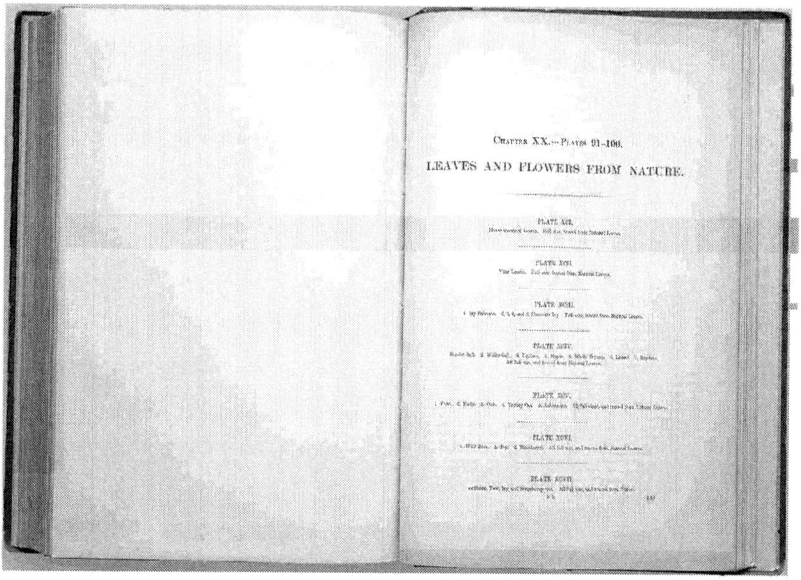

Chapter XX.—Plates 91–100.

LEAVES AND FLOWERS FROM NATURE.

PLATE XCI.

[illegible]

PLATE XCII.

Vine Leaves. Full size, traced from Natural Leaves.

PLATE XCIII.

[illegible]

PLATE XCIV.

[illegible]

PLATE XCV.

[illegible]

PLATE XCVI.

[illegible]

PLATE XCVII.

[illegible]

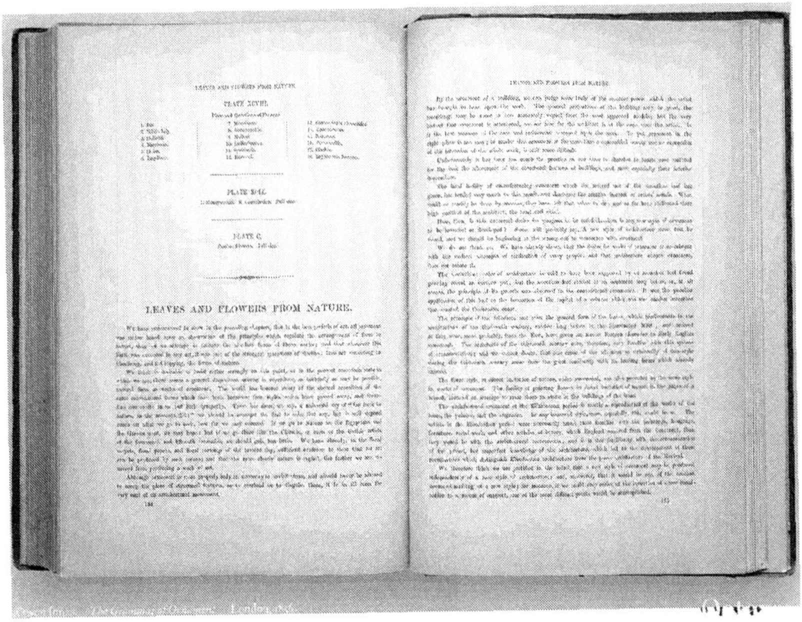

PLATE C.
LEAVES AND FLOWERS FROM NATURE.

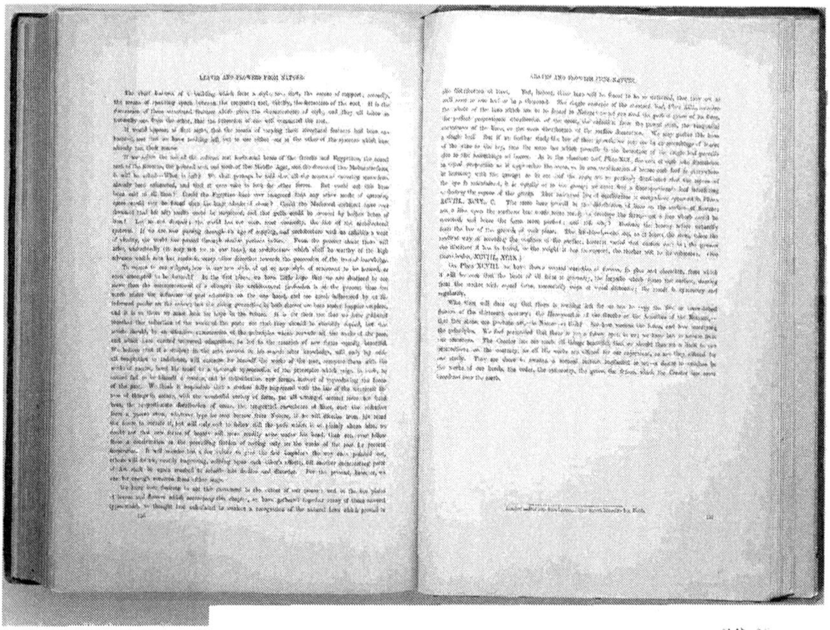

The chief features of a building which form a style, are, first, the means of support; secondly, the means of spanning space between the supports; and, thirdly, the formation of the roof. It is the [illegible] of these structural features which gives the characteristic of style, and they all follow so [illegible] one from the other, that the [illegible] of one will [illegible] the rest.

It would appear, at first sight, that the [illegible] of varying these structural features had been exhausted, and that we have nothing left but to use either one or the other of the systems which have already run their course. [illegible]

If we adopt the [illegible] of the columns and horizontal beams of the Greeks and Egyptians, the round arch of the Romans, the pointed arch and vault of the Middle Ages, and the domes of the Mohammedans, it will be asked—What is left? We shall perhaps be told that all the means of spanning space have already been exhausted, and that it were vain to look for other forms. But could not this have been said at all times? Could the Egyptian have ever imagined that any other mode of spanning space could ever be found than the huge blocks of stone? Could the Mediaeval architect have ever dreamed that his lofty vaults could be surpassed, and that [illegible] would be covered by hollow tubes of iron? [illegible] If we are now passing through an age of copying, and architecture with us exhibits a want of vitality, the world has passed through similar periods before. From the present chaos there will arise, undoubtedly (it may not be in our time), an architecture which shall be worthy of the high advance which man has made in every other direction towards the possession of the [illegible] knowledge.

To return to our subject, how is any new style of art or new style of ornament to be formed, or even attempted to be formed? In the first place, we have little hope that we are destined to see [illegible]

[illegible]

the distribution of lines. But, indeed, these laws will be found to be so universal, that they are as well seen in one leaf as in a thousand. The single example of the chestnut leaf, Plate XCI., contains the whole of the laws which are to be found in Nature: [illegible] the perfect proportionate distribution of the areas, the radiation from the parent stem, the tangential curvatures of the lines, [illegible] We may gather this from a single leaf. But if we further study the law of their growth, we [illegible] [illegible]

[illegible] XCVIII., XCIX., C. The same laws [illegible] in the distribution of lines on the surface of flowers [illegible] (See Plates, XCVIII., XCIX.)

On Plate XCVIII. we have drawn several varieties of flowers, in plan and elevation, from which it will be seen that the basis of all form is geometry, [illegible] symmetry and regularity.

Who then will dare say that there is nothing left for us but to copy the [illegible] flowers of the thirteenth century; the Honeysuckle of the Greeks or the Acanthus of the Romans,— that this alone can produce art,—is Nature so [illegible]? [illegible] The Creator has not made all things beautiful, that we should [illegible] [illegible] our study. They are there to awaken a natural instinct [illegible] in the works of our hands, the order, the symmetry, the grace, the fitness, which the Creator has [illegible] lavished over the earth.

[illegible]

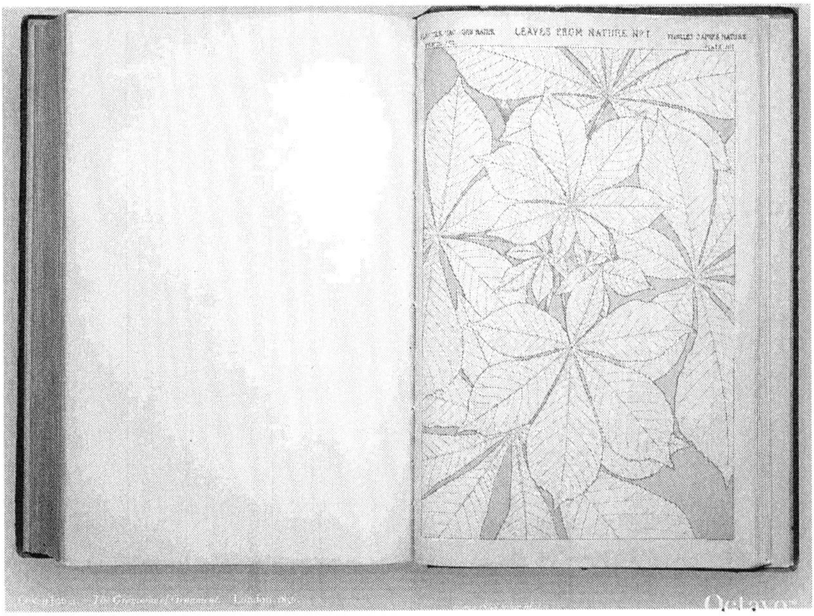
LEAVES FROM NATURE Nº 1

LEAVES FROM NATURE
Owen Jones The Grammar of Ornament London

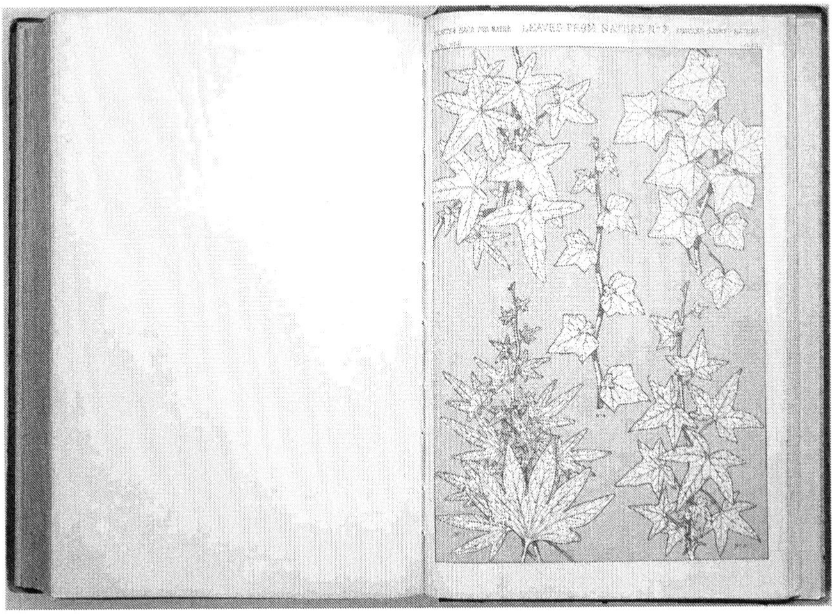
LEAVES FROM NATURE

LEAVES FROM NATURE

Owen Jones, The Grammar of Ornament, London 1856.

Owen Jones, *The Grammar of Ornament*, London, 1856

LEAVES FROM NATURE

Owen Jones: *The Grammar of Ornament*. London, 1856.

Owen Jones. *The Grammar of Ornament*. London, 1856.

Owen Jones *The Grammar of Ornament* London 1856

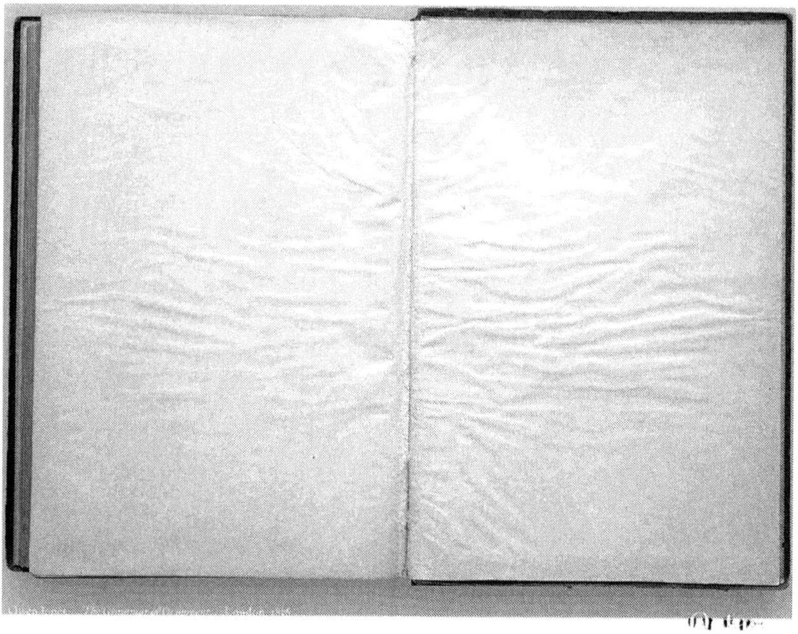

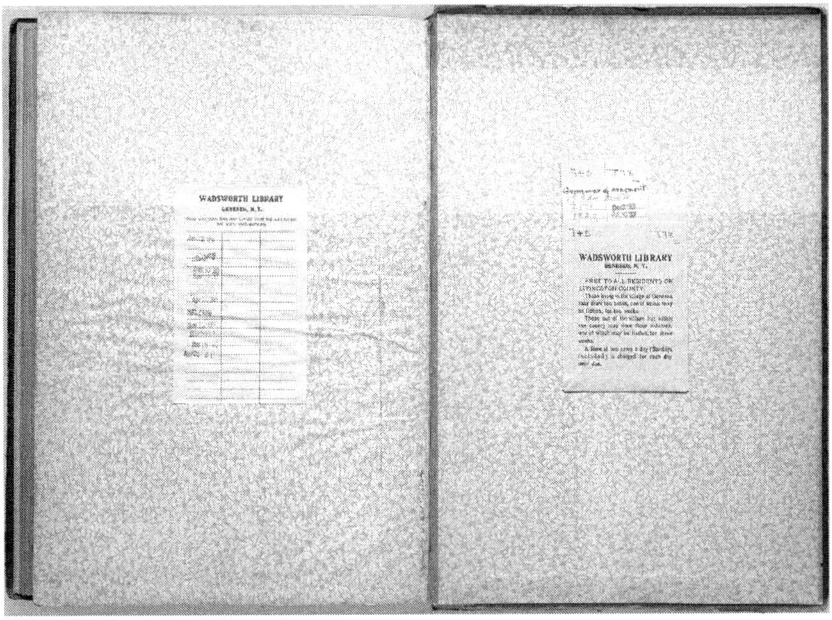
WADSWORTH LIBRARY
WADSWORTH LIBRARY

Milton Keynes UK
Ingram Content Group UK Ltd.
UKHW022033081123
432235UK00005B/106

9 781020 519710